GUID

CW01034006

Edited by **Rachel Tranter** and _Warburton_

BRF Ministries

15 The Chambers, Vineyard
Abingdon OX14 3FE
brf.org.uk | 01865 319700

Bible Reading Fellowship is a charity (233280)
and company limited by guarantee (301324),
registered in England and Wales

ISBN 978 1 80039 359 2
All rights reserved

This edition © Bible Reading Fellowship 2024
Cover image © Jakub/stock.adobe.com

Distributed in Australia by:
MediaCom Education Inc, PO Box 610, Unley, SA 5061
Tel: 1 800 811 311 | admin@mediacom.org.au

Distributed in New Zealand by:
Scripture Union Wholesale, PO Box 760, Wellington
Tel: 04 385 0421 | suwholesale@clear.net.nz

Acknowledgements
Scripture quotations marked with the following abbreviations are taken from the
version shown. Where no abbreviation is given, the quotation is taken from the
version stated in the contributor's introduction.

NRSV: the New Revised Standard Version Updated Edition. Copyright © 2021
National Council of Churches of Christ in the United States of America. Used
by permission. All rights reserved worldwide. NKJV: the New King James
Version®. Copyright © 1982 by Thomas Nelson. Used by permission. All rights
reserved. ISV: *The Holy Bible: International Standard Version*. Release 2.0, Build
2015.02.09. Copyright © 1995-2014 by ISV Foundation. ALL RIGHTS RESERVED
INTERNATIONALLY. Used by permission of Davidson Press, LLC. NIV: the Holy
Bible, New International Version (Anglicised edition) copyright © 1979, 1984, 2011
by Biblica. Used by permission of Hodder & Stoughton Publishers, a Hachette
UK company. All rights reserved. 'NIV' is a registered trademark of Biblica. UK
trademark number 1448790. NLT: the *Holy Bible*, New Living Translation, copyright
© 1996, 2004, 2015 by Tyndale House Foundation. Used by permission of Tyndale
House Publishers, Inc., Carol Stream, Illinois 60188. All rights reserved. AMP: The
Amplified Bible, copyright © 2015 by The Lockman Foundation, La Habra, CA
90631. All rights reserved. KJV: © public domain.

Every effort has been made to trace and contact copyright owners for material used
in this resource. We apologise for any inadvertent omissions or errors, and would
ask those concerned to contact us so that full acknowledgement can be made in
the future.

A catalogue record for this book is available from the British Library

Printed and bound in the UK by Zenith Media NP4 0DQ

Suggestions for using *Guidelines*

Set aside a regular time and place, if possible, when and where you can read and pray undisturbed. Before you begin, take time to be still and, if you find it helpful, use the BRF Ministries prayer on page 6.

In *Guidelines*, the introductory section provides context for the passages or themes to be studied, while the units of comment can be used daily, weekly or whatever best fits your timetable. You will need a Bible (more than one if you want to compare different translations) as Bible passages are not included. Please don't be tempted to skip the Bible reading because you know the passage well. We will have utterly failed if we don't bring our readers into engagement with the word of God. At the end of each week is a 'Guidelines' section, offering further thoughts about, or practical application of, what you have been studying.

Occasionally, you may read something in *Guidelines* that you find particularly challenging, even uncomfortable. This is inevitable in a series of notes which draws on a wide spectrum of contributors and doesn't believe in ducking difficult issues. Indeed, we believe that *Guidelines* readers much prefer thought-provoking material to a bland diet that only confirms what they already think.

If you do disagree with a contributor, you may find it helpful to go through these three steps. First, think about why you feel uncomfortable. Perhaps this is an idea that is new to you, or you are not happy about the way something has been expressed. Or there may be something more substantial – you may feel that the writer is guilty of sweeping generalisation, factual error, or theological or ethical misjudgement. Second, pray that God would use this disagreement to teach you more about his word and about yourself. Third, have a deeper read about the issue. There are further reading suggestions at the end of each writer's block of notes. And then, do feel free to write to the contributor or the editor of *Guidelines*. We welcome communication, by email, phone or letter, as it enables us to discover what has been useful, challenging or infuriating for our readers. We don't always promise to change things, but we will always listen and think about your ideas, complaints or suggestions. Thank you!

To send feedback, please email **enquiries@brf.org.uk**, phone **+44 (0)1865 319700** or write to the address shown opposite.

Writers in this issue

Walter Moberly is emeritus professor of theology and biblical interpretation at Durham University. He has recently written *The Bible in a Disenchanted Age* and *The God of the Old Testament* (both published by Baker Academic).

Sharon Prentis is deputy director of the Church of England's Racial Justice Unit (RJU). Prior to joining the RJU, she was dean of ministry at St Mellitus Theological College. Sharon has also served as a priest and is a vocal advocate for authentic leadership and justice.

Valerie Hobbs is a linguist at the University of Sheffield and author of *An Introduction to Religious Language* and *No Love in War: A story of Christian nationalism*. In her spare time, she writes about the Bible at **lampofthelamb.com**.

Victoria Omotoso is a cross-cultural research scholar whose work explores post-colonial discourse through biblical reception. She is an honorary research fellow at the University of Exeter, a tutor at the University of Southampton and a visiting lecturer at Sarum College and the London School of Theology.

Peter Hatton is a former tutor at Bristol Baptist College, where he taught after 25 years in Methodist ministry. Preaching, continuing teaching, writing projects and looking after grandchildren are keeping him occupied in 'retirement'.

Siobhán Jolley is a specialist in the portrayal of Mary Magdalene. She is a research fellow in art and religion at the National Gallery, visiting lecturer at King's College, London, and an honorary research fellow at the University of Manchester.

David Spriggs has been a Baptist Minister for over 50 years, serving in six different churches. For 20 of those years, he worked for the Evangelical Alliance and Bible Society. He has three married children and ten grandchildren.

M. J. Kramer is chaplain of Keble College, Oxford, having previously served as precentor of Canterbury Cathedral. His academic interests include classics, biblical studies, and Hellenistic Judaism. He is also author of *The Canterbury Book of New Parish Prayers*.

Loveday C. A. Alexander is professor emerita of biblical studies at the University of Sheffield, and canon-theologian emerita of Chester Cathedral. She is currently serving as a parish priest in Chester Diocese.

Andrew Smith is the director of interfaith relations for the bishop of Birmingham and founded the youth charity The Feast. He has been involved in various interfaith ministry since the mid-1990s.

The editors write…

Welcome to this new issue of *Guidelines* as we enter a new year!

In this issue, we continue our study of Luke alongside Loveday Alexander. Taking us through from the end of Jesus' teaching ministry in Galilee to the resurrection, Loveday helps us to see the cost of the path of peace that Jesus must tread. Max Kramer also travels with us on our journey through Lent with his notes on dealing with difficulty: how can the sufferings we observe in the Bible help shape how we understand the relationship between suffering and God, others, and ourselves? Meanwhile, Sharon Prentis helps us to see the joy of living for Christ in her notes on Philippians.

In the Old Testament, we study Leviticus, a book which many of us may regard with either dread or indifference! Peter Hatton helps us through this difficult book to see its countercultural encouragement towards holiness. Walter Moberly helps us to read and understand Nehemiah, which takes place at a time when those who followed God felt decentralised and irrelevant – a timely parallel to post-Christendom today. Following our series on New Testament prayers in the previous issue, Valerie Hobbs takes us through a series on Old Testament prayers, helping us to resist the dominant culture of neoliberalism and pray in a way that honours God rather than ourselves.

Two further timely sets of notes encourage us to think about relevant issues. Andrew Smith's notes on multifaith engagement help us to position ourselves in a world where the numbers of those following other faiths are rising much faster than Christianity. How do we engage with people of other faiths with integrity and respect? Meanwhile, Victoria Omotoso looks at the important topic of faith and culture, taking seriously Jesus' prayer in John 17 for unity alongside holiness.

Finally, David Spriggs gives us a fascinating series on Christian giving, while Siobhán Jolley brings us a new perspective on the much-maligned character of Mary Magdalene.

As ever, all of our contributors aim to bring you closer to the person and love of God.

Rachel   *Olivia*

The prayer of BRF Ministries

Faithful God,
thank you for growing BRF Ministries
from small beginnings
into the worldwide family it is today.
We rejoice as young and old
discover you through your word
and grow daily in faith and love.
Keep us humble in your service,
ambitious for your glory
and open to new opportunities.
For your name's sake.
Amen.

Helping to pay it forward

As part of our Living Faith ministry, we're raising funds to give away copies of Bible reading notes and other resources to those who aren't able to access them any other way, working with food banks and chaplaincy services, in prisons, hospitals and care homes.

'This very generous gift will be hugely appreciated, and truly bless each recipient… Bless you for your kindness.'

'We would like to send our enormous thanks to all involved. Your generosity will have a significant impact and will help us to continue to provide support to local people in crisis, and for this we cannot thank you enough.'

If you've enjoyed and benefited from our resources, would you consider paying it forward to enable others to do so too?

Make a gift at **brf.org.uk/donate**

Nehemiah: rebuilding the ruins

Walter Moberly

The main action of the book of Nehemiah takes place in Jerusalem, in the year 445BC (in our calendar; in ancient terms, the twentieth year of Artaxerxes).

The setting is the world of the Persian Empire, which succeeded the Babylonian Empire, and was a superpower in its day. Under King Cyrus in the 530s BC, the people of Judah, mostly in exile in Babylon, had been permitted to return to their land and resettle in and around Jerusalem. Although the temple was rebuilt, and initial expectations were high, as we see in Haggai and Zechariah, overall the restoration was disappointing; things didn't take off as hoped. The glory days of Israel and Judah (such as they were – it was always a mixed bag) were in the past. There was no longer a king from the house of David, for kings were not permitted to minor provinces in the Persian Empire, such as Judah now was. There was also a lack of good leaders to energise and guide people under God.

Two exceptions, however, were Ezra, a priest, and Nehemiah. Both found favour with the Persian ruler, King Artaxerxes, which they each ascribe to God's overruling. Artaxerxes authorised them to do further restoration in run-down Jerusalem. The precise relationship between the work of Ezra and Nehemiah is not specified in the books named after each. Nonetheless, as we will see, at a key moment they are presented together as enabling God's work of restoration.

There are certain resonances with the situation of the Christian churches in the post-Christian west, where the glory days (also a mixed bag) are in the past, and there is a struggle to remain faithful and get a hearing in a largely indifferent and uncomprehending culture. Nonetheless, we live in hope.

Unless otherwise stated, Bible quotations are taken from the NRSV.

1 The first response to a problem is prayer

Nehemiah 1

A distinctive feature of much of the narrative is that it is spoken by Nehemiah in his own first-person voice, presumably representing some kind of memoir. He gives minimal information about himself, beyond the fact that he had an honorific senior position as cupbearer in the royal court, which gave him access to the king (v. 11). The prime background information for what follows is the dire situation to which Jerusalem has been reduced (vv. 1–3).

Nehemiah's response to the grievous news is to channel his grief constructively by turning to God in prayer. Initially, the seriousness of the situation requires fasting, going without normal provision – a voluntary deprivation which symbolises and enables a deeper engagement with God (v. 4): deeper because it is costly.

Notably, the thought and language of his prayer is steeped in that of the book of Deuteronomy. (Compare, for example, v. 5 with Deuteronomy 7:9; 21, or vv. 8–9 with Deuteronomy 4:27; 30:1–4.) The implication is that Nehemiah was a faithful student of Israel's existing scripture, who had immersed himself in its content and made it his own. In his prayer he did not let his grief, which set the context, also set the tone, but rather he used scripture to form his understanding of, and approach to, God.

As a result, his initial note is that of acknowledging failure of faithfulness, both on the part of Israel as a whole and on his own part (vv. 6–7). They have failed to be and do what they should have, and so can have no claim on God: 'Nothing in my hands I bring', in the resonant words of Toplady's 'Rock of ages' hymn. Yet alongside this is the knowledge that the God who has called Israel is faithful beyond their failure, and so can be approached with confident hope (vv. 8–10). Indeed, Nehemiah mentions others, presumably summoned by him in this urgent situation, who also pray (in effect), 'Hallowed be thy name' (v. 11a). There are always some who remain faithful.

The focus of the prayer is not simply for vague, non-specific hopes of forgiveness and renewal; rather, it is intensely practical. Power arrangements on earth are real and make a difference. So, Nehemiah asks the Lord to hear him favourably in heaven so that he may receive a favourable hearing on earth with the person of power, the king (v. 11). Practicalities matter.

2 Public and personal realities

Nehemiah, and those praying with him, have prayed for about four months, from Chislev (1:1, early winter) to Nisan (v. 1, early spring). Patience sets the context for this moment of opportunity, when the king takes a personal, and perceptive, interest in his cupbearer (vv. 1–2). Nehemiah observes formal propriety ('may the king live forever' is a strong form of 'long live the king') and speaks of human loss in a way that a king could appreciate (v. 3). The king comes straight to the point, and Nehemiah, with an arrow prayer for God's overruling at this key moment, responds. In the months of prayer, he has clearly had time to think through the practicalities of what is needed, both in terms of time required (one imagines at least a year in the first instance) and the resources amd in terms of the bureaucracy of permits for Persian officials en route and substantial building materials. This is a big ask, but with God's gracious overruling, the king grants it and throws in a substantial military escort for good measure (vv. 4–8, 9).

Despite God's sovereign enabling, there is opposition (v. 10). Interestingly, we are given no background information as to why Sanballat and Tobiah should be hostile to Nehemiah (though plausible explanatory conjectures are of course possible). As the narrative stands, they simply *are* hostile. As such, the presentation of their hostility embodies that enduring mystery of life in God's world, that even if darkness does not overcome the light, darkness is still there and resists it. There may be no clear reason, but rather an ultimately inexplicable presence of evil in the human heart. Faith that does not reckon with this may easily be thrown into disarray.

Although Nehemiah now has an official role to rebuild Jerusalem, with the backing of the Persian king, he still needs quiet time to assess the situation. He has a sense of what God wants him to do (the NRSV's 'what my God had put into my heart' in v. 11 is misleading – the Hebrew verb is a present participle, 'putting', indicating that it is still in process). But he needs space and peace to work it through, under God. So he goes out at night with a few trusted companions (vv. 11–16). Night isn't a great time for viewing things, but one can reasonably imagine a full moon and good torches. These few hours, away from crowds and hassle, enable Nehemiah to get a clear and confident sense of the way ahead.

3 The difference a good leader can make

Nehemiah 2:17—3:14

Removing the shameful desolation of Jerusalem by rebuilding its shattered walls and gates may seem an obvious thing to do. Nonetheless, it would be an arduous task. Additionally, the politics of the Persian Empire could complicate matters. Nehemiah encourages and reassures his hearers by appealing to the good will of both God and the king, and thereby elicits their commitment to the task. But it remained possible to take it all in a suspicious and hostile way: the king's permission to Nehemiah didn't envisage *this* much and *really* it is all a covert bid for independence. Nehemiah does not waste time arguing. He just tells his opponents that they are excluding themselves from God's good purposes for his people (2:17–20).

Chapter 3 offers the first of a number of detailed and extensive lists of people that characterise the book of Nehemiah. Such lists are not obviously engaging for the contemporary reader. Yet although there are numerous interesting points of detail, part of their significance lies in seeing the list of names as a whole, as on a war memorial. There is some analogy to what one can see at many a football stadium, where there are often extensive walls of bricks, each inscribed with the name of a donor who wanted to support and be associated with that place. One can look for particular names ('Ooh, there's John/Jane') but one also needs to get a sense of the whole, the way in which people and place have come to belong together. Here we have the literary memorial of those who loved Jerusalem at a low point in its history.

One striking thing is how many people come out of the woodwork. These were people who already lived in and around Jerusalem, who had clearly got accustomed to its dismal state and had just been getting on with their lives as best they could. Nehemiah changes that. Now that he is giving a clear lead, having made the various necessary preparations, people respond and set to doing all that needs to be done (though sadly there are some whose petty pride resists the grace of a special moment, 3:5b).

It is worth noting that those who know the old city of Jerusalem should not try to relate this passage to the current walls and gates, as the layout has changed over its long history. But the hilly terrain remains a good imaginative guide to some of the challenges of rebuilding.

4 Persistence, persistence, persistence

Nehemiah 4

The opposition to Nehemiah's work initially takes the form of words, mocking words. These ridicule and seek to undermine morale, perhaps addressing secret fears in the minds of those who are rebuilding. Although Nehemiah had been equipped with wood (2:8), the provision of stone had to be local, and there was little recent experience of quarrying good stone. So, the early sections of rebuilt wall may indeed have looked unimpressive. But they wisely concentrated on joining up the sections of wall, rather than completing individual sections, so as to provide the best basic security. Nehemiah also responds with words of his own, wishing in prayer that the mockers could know for themselves what it was like to suffer the horrors of captivity and deportation, as so many of those they were mocking had done (vv. 1–6).

Then the opposition threatens action, specifically murderous military action in some form. So, henceforth, military preparedness has to become part of the task of rebuilding (vv. 7–23). It would have been awkward and slowed things down greatly. It may be why everybody involved in the rebuilding worked from as early as possible till as late as possible (v. 21) and Nehemiah and some companions only slept in such a way that they could instantly spring into action: weary and smelly, no doubt, but getting the job done.

Two keynotes are in verses 9 and 14. Verse 9 is a biblical formulation of the principle famously ascribed to Oliver Cromwell: 'Trust God and keep your powder dry'. Looking to God in prayer, as Nehemiah does, is basic. But it is no substitute for taking responsible action as well. Nehemiah's swords are equivalent to Cromwell's muskets. The principle is always valid (unless God specifies inaction, as in 2 Chronicles 20:17), even though its outworking for us today will be far removed from both swords and muskets. Trust God, and revise for the exam; trust God, and keep your accounts up to date; trust God, and don't drink before driving…

Verse 14 speaks of how best to deal with fear in a dangerous situation. First, look to God and remember his sovereign power. Secondly, remember those near and dear. In other words, we are not to think of ourselves, but rather of God and others. Loving focus on God and on neighbour is the healthy ordering of priorities when there is danger.

5 Leading by example

We now learn that the broken-down state of the city is matched by the broken-down state of many of its inhabitants. Food is scarce and so is money. People are having to riskily mortgage their basic means of livelihood (v. 3), borrow money not to feed themselves but to pay Persian taxes (v. 4) and even sell their children into slavery; though the end result is not an escape from their difficulties, but rather overall becoming ever more helplessly entrapped (v. 5).

What makes it so bad is that much of this is down to ruthless exploitation, not from the Persians but from their fellow-countrymen (vv. 6–13). Nehemiah is enraged when he learns what is going on and calls fellow Jews of wealth and power to account (and a prophet like Amos might have observed that in this, Nehemiah is displaying the attitude and priorities of their God). Nehemiah invokes the 'fear of God', a prime Old Testament term for right human response to God, which is regularly oriented specifically towards not taking advantage of those who are weaker than us and at our mercy (see e.g. Leviticus 19:14, where the vulnerable deaf and blind, who could be bad-mouthed and tripped up with apparent impunity, are to be treated with respect and restraint, summed up as 'fearing God'). Nehemiah demands no less than full restitution of everything that has been squeezed out of those struggling to survive. Yet he does not consider it sufficient to take people's word that they will do it (v. 12a); he knows that words can be cheap while greed goes deep in the human heart. He ups the stakes not only by exacting symbolically weighted words, an oath before the priests (representing God), but also by performing a symbolic action, akin to what many prophets did (see e.g. Isaiah 20:1–5), to depict God's judgement on the faithless. This still brings no guarantee of true response; but restitution does indeed take place.

Nehemiah also tells of how he went without the perks that came with his position as governor, the perks that always come to people with power (vv. 14–19). He refused to live in undue comfort while his people struggled. Again, he appeals to the 'fear of God' as his own reason for living thus. In important ways Nehemiah already understands and anticipates Jesus' definitive reformulation of the nature of power: not to be served, but to serve.

6 When suspicion is wise

Nehemiah 6:1—7:4

Nehemiah's opponents don't give up. Rather, they vary their strategy. Initially they invite Nehemiah for a meeting (6:1–4). This could sound like a constructive proposal to mend fences and find common ground, such that Nehemiah would look to be in the wrong to turn it down. But naivety is no virtue in a leader, and Nehemiah is rightly suspicious. This is likely an inference from their past behaviour, together with their not offering to meet Nehemiah on his own ground in Jerusalem. That kind of proposal, putting themselves at potential risk, would likely be a genuine overture.

This suspicion is confirmed by their next ploy, an open letter (whose contents would become public knowledge) which develops their earlier mockery (6:6–9, compare 2:19): it would be easy to present Nehemiah's work to the Persian king as covert rebellion. Again, Nehemiah simply gets on with his task (maybe trusting to his own knowledge of the Persian king) and prays for strength to complete it.

Others too, not previously known for hostility, join in conspiring against Nehemiah with warning of an imminent assassination attempt, such that Nehemiah needs to hide in the temple, Nehemiah instinctively refuses, as he is a man moulded by his fear of, i.e. faith in, God. This is analogous to Zelensky's celebrated words at the invasion of Ukraine, when offered an evacuation flight: 'I need ammunition, not a ride.' Faithfulness to responsibilities can be more important than personal safety. But this can be hard, especially when other people in responsible positions find no problem in abusing their role through financial inducement (6:10–14).

The completion of the wall leads to wide recognition that it had been completed against the odds, indeed with divine assistance. But alongside this, Nehemiah mentions yet further attempts to put him off: some nobles of Judah had strong social links with Tobiah, such that they talked up Tobiah and ratted on Nehemiah (6:15–19).

It is hardly surprising, therefore, that Nehemiah gives responsibility for the restored Jerusalem to people he knows and trusts. He also proceeds cautiously: no opening of the gates of Jerusalem till a time of day when people are generally up and about, and early closing while people were still around. Enemies were out there, and a thinly populated city needed to take care. Proceeding cautiously is never glamorous, but it may lay a foundation for good things in the future (7:1–4).

Guidelines

A distinctive feature of Nehemiah's first-person account is the inclusion of a number of short prayers, interjected into the narrative (and distinct from the long prayer in 1:5–11). Four of these we have already encountered – 4:4–5, 5:19, 6:9, 14 – and three come next week – 13:14, 22, 31. They interestingly stand out from the narrative of events, which is set in the past, by praying as though the moment in the narrative were still present. For both better and worse, the past can live in the present.

The tone of the prayers, however, can readily grate on the sensibilities of a Christian reader today. Imprecation on enemies (e.g. 4:4–5) feels to be some distance from 'Bless those who persecute you; bless and do not curse them' (Romans 12:14). Prayer for God to remember Nehemiah and what he has done (e.g. 5:19) can feel self-righteous and lacking in an understanding of grace, seeming closer to the Pharisee than to the tax collector (Luke 18:9–14).

To read the Old Testament as scripture, still authoritative for today, does not mean supposing that everything in it is of equal value. Nor does it entail that Nehemiah, with his undoubted living knowledge of God, should have understood God's ways to the same depth that is possible in the light of Christ crucified and risen. Neither scripture nor the life of faith is an 'all or nothing' affair, but rather a rich reality with many distinctions and gradations. But if Christians have been given a fuller knowledge of God, we should remember that much is expected of those to whom much is given. If we can know God more fully than Nehemiah, are we serving God more fully and more faithfully?

Some ancient Greek manuscripts at Nehemiah 1:11 say that Nehemiah was a eunuch. Whether this was so we cannot be sure; it's not in the Hebrew original. But it might make sense of his tone in a culture that particularly looked to God's future blessing in terms of children and descendants, from which, as a eunuch, he would have been excluded. Those of us who live securely should not look down on those whose speech reflects their being wounded and vulnerable. God knows the reality of the heart, and answers prayer accordingly.

1 Tears and joy

Nehemiah 8

We have passed over another literary memorial to those who had repopulated Jerusalem and Judah after the exile. This memorial is for the most part identical to Ezra 2, apparently taken from an archive (7:5–73).

We now witness a great gathering in Jerusalem for the reading of the 'law' (7:73b—8:12) – though 'teaching' or 'instruction' better convey the sense of the underlying Hebrew term, *Torah*, as Israel's scripture is to instruct the people in God's will and purposes for them. One surprise is the presence of Ezra, who has not previously been mentioned by Nehemiah. Yet clearly, we are to envisage these two leaders, governor and priest, as both integral to this time of renewal (8:9).

Alongside Ezra leading the reading and prayer, Levites help with issues of interpretation and understanding (vv. 7–8). This was not quite the modern phenomenon of simultaneous translation, but probably involved qualified teachers moving among the people, clarifying the sense of the reading.

The people are deeply moved by what they hear, which hitherto had clearly been too little known or heeded (vv. 9–12). Their tears might be repentance but perhaps more likely express sorrowing wonder at all they had been missing out on. As the Cabby says at the founding of Narnia: 'Glory be! I'd ha' been a better man all my life if I'd known there were things like this' (*The Magician's Nephew*, C.S. Lewis). The authoritative guidance from the platform is clear: the day is holy, and this must be understood as a cause, not of sorrow, but rather of joy and celebration. Joy at re-engaging with God's will for them as his people will best enable standing firm in living as they should (8:10).

Further study of the teaching brings a reminder of the importance of the festival of booths (vv. 13–18), as prescribed in Leviticus 23:39–44. This commemorated Israel's living in booths after leaving Egypt (Leviticus 23:43), a symbolic reminder of their being a pilgrim people, dependent on God's provision, even when settled in Jerusalem. The festival had not entirely fallen out of practice (see Ezra 3:4), but perhaps the full-blown camping out had not been observed. Now full observance of a ceremony that symbolises their identity as God's people brings further joy; they are steadily being restored to being the people they were called to be.

2 Heart-searching and confession

Nehemiah 9:1–37

The restoration of the people of Jerusalem as the people of the Lord is a many-sided reality, in which hands and mind and conscience and spirit are all involved. The rebuilding of the wall had to be complemented by the cancelling of exploitative financial dealings (chapters 4—5). The renewed understanding of scripture and observance of a symbolic festival (chapter 8) needs now to be complemented by a heart-searching turning to God in prayer (chapter 9).

It is clearly an arduous and demanding occasion, as two quarters of the day would be about six hours (v. 3). Some Levites set the initial tone with blessing God's name, which means a combination of thanksgiving and setting their hearts and minds on God ('hallowed be your name'). As Ezra read out scripture previously, now he leads in a long prayer that looks back over Israel's story as a whole, starting with the initial call of Abraham by the sovereign creator God (vv. 6–8).

There is a strong contrast between 'you', the God to whom they are praying who has consistently acted graciously and generously, and 'they', Abraham's descendants who received so much from God and yet would not respond in trust and obedience (vv. 9–17a). And this contrast of generosity and unresponsiveness plays out yet again in a similar way (vv. 17b–26). This changes to divine judgement, cries of suffering, divine deliverance and then a renewed faithlessness immediately repeats the pattern (vv. 27–31).

The past leads up to and continues in the present in the climactic 'Now therefore… today' (v. 32). The keynotes of God's faithfulness and the people's faithlessness lead into the painful paradox: the people are back in the land given by God – and yet they are in effect slaves, subject to the exploitations of the Persians. The land of gift and freedom has become the land of oppression and distress (vv. 36–37).

The prayer as a whole is sobering. There is acknowledgment of the relentlessly self-serving nature of those whom God has called to a different and better way of living. There is recognition that the gift of God can be turned into misery. Although God's goodness remains the bottom line, human heedlessness can nullify the life and joy it should bring. As we will see tomorrow, this is not the end, but the basis for a new beginning. Yet without this painful self-knowledge, there will be no new beginning.

3 A pledge for the future

On the basis of the prayer of confession, Nehemiah and other leaders with him produce a written pledge, which they sign and seal (9:38—10:27). This will be the basis for a future which they long to be different from the past. Others also join with them in a solemn commitment, where the 'curse and oath' (10:29) means that there will be sanctions and penalties for failure to live up to this undertaking.

The pledge involves not moral and spiritual generalities but practical specifics. First, no intermarriage with those who are not part of Judah (10:30). This is because marriage in premodern societies was not just two individuals getting together, but rather a matter of familial interaction and cultural embrace, such that marriage into families who did not acknowledge the Lord God would compromise Judah's own allegiance.

Secondly, no trading on the sabbath (10:31a). This is to preserve a deep symbolic marker of the people's allegiance to God, whereby on a holy day business is set aside. Time, like money, is subject to a tithe, here in the joyful form of a weekly holiday.

Thirdly, this Sabbath tithe is to be extended to crops of the seventh year and debt remission. Money and profit are not to be an unqualified good in the community.

Beyond these initial commitments, all the rest relate to provision for Jerusalem's temple, the place of worship that is the symbolic centre of their life (10:32–39, summarised in the final words of 10:39). For us, living in a secularised society which is inclined to marginalise religion as insignificant and best kept private, it can be difficult to appreciate the importance of the temple. In our terms it would be something like Westminster for the politician, the City for the financier and Wembley for the sportsperson, only all in one!

The provisions for the temple in various ways go beyond what is specified in the Mosaic commandments, showing realistic appreciation of how practices need to develop in order to continue to do what needs to be done. So, for example, there is no scriptural specification of a tax for the upkeep of the sanctuary (10:32–33), nor is there any specification of a wood offering (10:34). But money and wood (for offerings by fire) are both necessary and appropriate. Our use of our resources in God's service needs likewise to be serious.

4 A time to celebrate

Again, we pass over another literary memorial to those who repopulated Judah and Jerusalem (11:1—12:26). This one focuses especially on the clergy, the priests and Levites, because of the importance of the temple in the restored Jerusalem.

We return to the city wall, the completion of whose rebuilding had been noted previously (6:15). Interestingly, there is also the reappearance of Nehemiah's first-person voice (12:31), which has not been heard since 7:5. In the meantime, a narrator has spoken of Nehemiah in the third person (8:9, 10:1), which is no doubt indicative of the book being composed both from Nehemiah's own memoir and from materials from a Jerusalem archive. The rebuilt wall is now dedicated with a great celebration, both as a marker of what has been possible with God's help and as a marker of the future special status of Jerusalem as a, indeed *the*, 'holy city' (11:1).

The first step is purification, both of people and of fabric (v. 30). We are not told what this involved. It may have been an early example of what has since become common Christian practice, sprinkling with water, as water is an obvious and accessible symbol of being cleansed in God's sight and open to him. Symbols may sometimes be trivial, but they can also matter.

Then there are two great processions, which together walk round the circuit of the restored wall, each covering half and then meeting up (vv. 31–43). This symbolically enacts the people's possession of the city as a whole and their recognition of it as a special place of God's presence in the temple. Psalm 48 suggests that this may perhaps have been a regular practice in Jerusalem's history and encourages people to walk round Jerusalem's walls with a view to celebrating the presence of God in this place (Psalm 48:12–14). Indeed, Psalm 48 might well have been one of the songs sung in Nehemiah's dedication, in which music and singing was prominent (v. 27). The final note is emphatically 'joy' (the Hebrew word, as both verb and noun, comes five times in v. 43).

Joyful celebrations of special moments, not least those for which one has worked – say, in education, or training, or public service – matter. In an age of informality, people sometimes don't bother. But we can be impoverished by their lack. A focus on special moments, to thank God for what has been possible, can help enhance and hallow our appreciation of the mundane moments also.

5 Fulfilling mundane responsibilities

Nehemiah 12:44—13:3

One might perhaps feel that the book of Nehemiah could and should have ended at 12:43, for that strong note of joy in Jerusalem would make for ending on a high. But, as we know, life is not like that. Highs are important and should be made the most of. But daily and mundane practical concerns never go away, and still need attending to. So, we have two notes about everyday issues, which are closely associated with the joyful dedication of the wall 'on that day' (12:44, 13:1).

First is the appointment of people to oversee the temple's storerooms, which were needed for offerings brought to Jerusalem (12:44–47). There is a particular perennial problem. When people – priests and Levites – are devoted to the service of God, they no longer do the kind of productive work that generates an income to live on. In the Old Testament, this is symbolised by the tribe of Levi not receiving a portion of territory like all the other tribes of Israel, and thereby lacking regular means of sustenance (Deuteronomy 10:9). This means that if they are not to starve, they must live off offerings brought by members of other tribes when they come to the temple, some of which needs storing. Likewise today, clergy, religious and Christian workers are a rough equivalent to ancient priests and Levites; and the faithful must give their money so that they have the necessaries to live on. Strikingly in our passage, Judah 'rejoiced' over their clergy, as part of the wider rejoicing at the restoration of Jerusalem. May such joy be present in church life today.

Secondly, further scriptural reading drew attention to Deuteronomy 23:3–5, which prohibits Ammonites and Moabites from being part of Israel (13:1–3). This is interpreted as involving a principle about 'those of foreign descent' generally, and some sort of separation is directly enacted. The form of the separation is not specified, and it may not be the break-up of mixed marriages as in Ezra 9—10, but rather exclusion from festivals such as the just-mentioned dedication of the wall. The concern for faithfulness is clear. Nonetheless, a reader of the Old Testament as a whole cannot but be aware that it contains other voices, most notably the book of Ruth, where a Moabite woman embraces Israel's life and Israel's God and thereby becomes the great-grandmother of King David. Faithfulness must remain alert and attentive.

6 The struggle does not cease

Nehemiah 13:4–30

If only the high moments, and the making of good arrangements, could be long lasting. The final part of Nehemiah brings us down to earth with a bump, as we see three areas, which Nehemiah had already dealt with, as either unravelling or unsettled.

First, the temple (vv. 4–14): part of the temple's storerooms, necessary for provisions for the clergy, had been allowed to become niche accommodation for one of Nehemiah's opponents from earlier in the book, Tobiah (vv. 4–9). This had only been possible because Nehemiah had been out of town for a while on a dutiful visit back to Susa to the Persian king. On his return, Nehemiah wastes no time in despatching Tobiah, purifying the space and returning it to its proper purpose. In a more modest way, it's reminiscent of Israel making a golden calf as soon as Moses' back is turned (Exodus 32). How long does it take for God's people to learn to live responsibly?

Relatedly, the necessary provisions for the clergy had not been forthcoming, so some of them had had to leave the temple and go and work the ground to keep themselves and their families alive (vv. 10–14). Again, Nehemiah intervenes and appoints new officials, who have a reputation for the all-important quality of being faithful, so that this should not happen again.

Secondly, sabbath observance (vv. 15–22), which was part of the pledge (10:31). This is one of the commandments most easily neglected in the pursuit of the apparent convenience of daily 'business as usual'. Prophets like Amos and Jeremiah had spoken out against ignoring the sabbath, possibly with limited effect (Amos 8:5, Jeremiah 17:19–27). It is surely a paradox that God's gift of weekly space and time should be so easily overridden; life with God means learning patterns of living that do not necessarily come easily.

Thirdly, mixed marriages (vv. 23–31): as already noted (day 3), the core issue is resisting practices, in marriage and the upbringing of children, that diminish faithful adherence to the way of the Lord.

Each of these three sections concludes with a prayer by Nehemiah. Nehemiah, perhaps aware of the possible frailty of his arrangements, and of his own transience in relation to Judah's future, prays that his faithfulness in all these matters will be heeded by God. The note he sounds may jar somewhat. Yet the principle that faithfulness is more important than success is basic to scripture and Christian life.

Guidelines

A problematic mindset of many in the modern west is to make a sharp division between the material and the spiritual. In certain ways this is rooted in the Enlightenment tendency to privilege the material world, on which the natural sciences could work successfully, over the spiritual, which was inaccessible to the natural sciences and so all too easily downplayed as merely subjective and fanciful. One of the marks of a 'postmodern' phase is an unease with this division, and a common desire to recover the 'spiritual', yet without really knowing how to go about handling the issues well.

Here scripture is foundational, as it refuses this division as usually understood. It makes clear that the spiritual has a name and a face, and that there is a map for understanding its main contours. In this regard, the book of Nehemiah has a significant voice, for Christians as well as for others.

For example, we might think that moral and spiritual change should always come first. Yet in Nehemiah the rebuilding of the walls of Jerusalem comes first. The implication is that certain public and material practices can symbolise and enable the changing of heart and mind. Nehemiah's leadership draws people out over time, and the first step is to attend to the security of walls, not at the expense of, but rather as integral to, a larger renewal.

Alternatively, when scripture is read out by Ezra and hearts and minds are touched deeply, initial sorrow gives way, through wise teaching, to joy in the wonders of the Lord and his ways. Yet joy is also emphasised at the celebratory dedication of the rebuilt wall. Scripture is deeper and more enduring than a rebuilt wall, but both have a major place in Nehemiah's narrative.

Finally, and slightly differently, it is easy to assume that spiritual people should always be enticing people. But is this so? How many of the great saints of the church would have been good company at a dinner party? St Francis of Assisi would not even have accepted the invitation in the first place! Jesus is in many ways exceptional in this regard. The real attraction of the spiritual realm should be faithfulness to the Lord and his ways. Nehemiah, a somewhat forbidding figure, reminds us that this can rightly take many forms, and that we need to learn to recognise where true value is present.

FURTHER READING

Timothy Escott, *Faithfulness & Restoration: Towards reading Ezra–Nehemiah as Christian scripture* (Wipf & Stock, 2023)

Derek Kidner, *Ezra and Nehemiah* (IVP: 2024 [originally 1979])

H.G.M. Williamson, *Ezra, Nehemiah* (Thomas Nelson, 1986)

Philippians: the joy of living for Christ

Sharon Prentis

Sometimes it can feel hard to be joyful in the midst of life's challenges. Individual experiences, not to mention the state of the world we live in, can make joy seem elusive or inappropriate. Nevertheless, the joy referred to in the Bible comes from the belief that no matter what happens, God is always present and working out all things for good. The psalmist proclaimed, 'Weeping may endure for a night, but joy comes in the morning' (Psalm 30:5, NKJV), and this perspective can help us find peace and hope amid even the most troubling of situations. The book of Philippians is often referred to as a letter of joy, written for times when courage and strength was particularly needed. It was written to encourage the original hearers to remain faithful, pursue the person and power of Jesus Christ, and appreciate how the knowledge of him brings peace and emboldens lives. Over the next two weeks, we will explore the truths presented in this letter, to increase our understanding of what it means to live in joy during tough times and the joy that comes from seeking God with all our heart (Jeremiah 29:13). Through the apostle Paul's writings, we are encouraged to express joy in the proclamation of Jesus Christ as Lord in whatever situations we find ourselves. The challenge here is to focus on the Messiah as redeemer and his message of hope, not on anything else. Paul's proclamation, 'to live is Christ' (1:21), reminds us to view our current circumstances from an eternal perspective, with the knowledge that we are never alone.

On some occasions, passages have been revisited to draw out different perspectives. Unless otherwise stated, Bible quotations are taken from the NKJV.

1 Finding joy when others share

Philippians 1:1–18

In this rousing opening to Paul's letter to the church in Philippi, the word joy, which goes on to be a significant theme, is mentioned for the first time (Philippians 1:4). Together with its verbal form, rejoice, it will be used over 14 times in this letter, more often than in any other of Paul's letters. Paul writes to express his gratitude to God for the people of Philippi who have generously supported his ministry. He does this by praying for their well-being and growth as followers of Jesus Christ and by encouraging them through teaching the faith. His focus is on others rather than on himself; in this way, Paul encourages leaders to look beyond their immediate personal concerns to those in their care, reminding them of God's proximity and provision, which is often through the generosity of others. His expression of gratitude is for financial support, other resources and prayer, to further the spread of the gospel. The generosity of those who give demonstrates unity in both purpose and mission.

Praying for others means more than solely interceding and pleading to God on their behalf. It also involves giving thanks to God for them, a consistent theme in Paul's letters. In his correspondence with the Ephesians, he thanks those who have supported him and for whom he feels particular concern (Ephesians 1:15–16). By doing this, he combines thanksgiving and joy; there is no hierarchical relationship, but rather a deep appreciation for the community. Even when correcting them, Paul encourages them to be better. Gratitude is not measured in banal clichés, but rather a sense of wonder at what God is doing among his people. This is the strength of our joy: it is connected to the promotion of the gospel rather than to our circumstances or the reactions of others to us. Joy in the Lord remains constant, even during challenges. Paul could be joyful not only towards those filled with goodwill and love towards him, but also towards those who preached the gospel out of rivalry and contempt for him. In community, what this speaks to is that our focus should be orientated towards joy and not towards scrutinising the motives of those involved in sharing the gospel. Our prayers then become shaped by thanksgiving that Christ is known.

2 Being sent for a purpose

Philippians 1:1–18

The word 'apostle' comes from the Greek *apostolos*, meaning 'one who is sent out'. The associated Latin expression is *mission*, 'sending'; and the gospel message of the early church was conveyed by those who were being sent across the world in accordance with Christ's command to make disciples of all nations (Matthew 28:19). There were many different types of apostles with various tasks of ministry, support, encouragement and to live out the mission, often in places hostile to the message of the coming kingdom and the lordship of Jesus Christ. The early Christians were well aware that they were the subject of intense societal suspicion ranging from undertaking strange practices such as the Lord's Supper all the way up to subverting the state and disloyalty to the emperor. As a result, they experienced oppression, and yet the early church thrived. An important characteristic of Pauline theology is highlighting that God works through adverse circumstances, choosing the foolishness of the cross to redeem a fallen humanity (1:27). As it was then and is now, suffering for the gospel's sake is a reality for a significant number of Christians throughout the world. In identifying with Christ and with Paul, the Philippians share in their afflictions. God's name is still being praised despite their circumstances, and Jesus is being glorified, because of their witness to the gospel.

The life-enhancing, freeing gospel of Jesus Christ is the main point; in verses 15–18 Paul explains that even though some may preach the gospel from selfish ambition, it is not our task to judge but to believe in God, who is the subject of the gospel being preached. Therefore, the name of the Lord will be praised regardless. Moreover, our joy is compounded as we rejoice together, thanks to the triumph of Jesus over sin and death. Comparing this joy to current culture understandings of joy, one can see that it is not fleeting or dependent on external circumstances. It is a deep and abiding joy that comes from knowing Christ. The confidence that comes from assurance in Christ cannot then be diminished by affliction, and the purpose for which Paul was sent out will prevail.

3 A faith to die and live for

Philippians 1:19–30

The Christian pastor and theologian Dietrich Bonhoeffer was executed during World War II for resisting Nazi dictatorship. His final message reflected an understanding that he would inevitably face execution, but his death, because of Christ, was not the final chapter when viewed from the perspective of eternity. As a founding member of the Confessing Church in Germany, which resisted attempts to elevate Nazi ideology over Christian doctrine, Bonhoeffer declared there was more to life than this current existence. His attitude highlighted victory through faith.

At times of great turmoil, the question of how we live for the gospel is particularly acute. The apostle Paul did everything he could to spread and encourage the gospel message. He asserts that his death is a net gain because it allows him to be with Christ, which he considers 'far better' than living (1:21–23). This way of looking at life serves not only as a strategy for Paul to endure the present trials of arrest and prison, but also as a message of hope for the Philippians. Despite the threat from imperial Roman's ability to destroy his body, Paul views his death instead as a glorious moment of reunion with Christ (v. 23). Paul's view turns worldly priorities upside down. Material possessions and activities focused on self-indulgence lose their appeal compared to the hope of being with Christ. Living life in Christ takes on new meaning when rooted in faith rather than being considered from more natural, fear-driven perspectives. Even in prison, Paul did not stop preaching Christ, crucified and risen. Thus, Paul's imprisonment inspired confidence within other Christians to talk about Jesus more openly and optimistically. Either scenario had merit. Even though the possibility of imprisonment and execution was apparent, real life is defined by following the Messiah. Dying would mean being present with Jesus, which would be a bonus for him. If released, he could keep working to start more Jesus-shaped communities, which would be better for others. Dying for Jesus is not the true sacrifice, it's staying alive to serve others. This is what participating in the story of Jesus – to suffer and to love others more than ourselves – truly means.

4 Current troubles in the context of future hope

Philippians 1:19–30

There is a human tendency to think of time as linear, so that our life is focused on the present with only intermittent references to the past or the future. The current trend for mindfulness is to promote awareness in the moment. However, for Paul, the gospel message is concerned not only with current circumstances but those yet to come in the ongoing revelation of the kingdom. In this letter, the future and the present are considered simultaneously; we see his perspective on what's happening now and as it relates to the future. Paul presents the challenge of living out hope in the present while being orientated towards the culmination which will come, all while enduring hardships.

The reality is that if we forget the future dimension of the gospel, we forget the summation of the gospel itself and the hope it contains to ensure the transformation of all things. In this way the Philippians' suffering has Christological significance; they suffer on behalf of Christ (1:29). Paul encourages the Philippians to stand firm together, united in spirit and purpose (v. 27). His words emphasise the body of Christ, the church where believers support and care for one another, prioritise the gospel and bless those who are yet to have a personal relationship with the Messiah. Participating in others' suffering is part of being the body of Christ. Suffering for the sake of Christ is not only a sign of our commitment to him but also a way of participating in his redemptive story. By embracing both the present challenges and the future hope of the gospel, we can live out our faith authentically and courageously, knowing that our ultimate citizenship is in heaven and our ultimate hope is in Christ. By adopting the same mindset, our lives as citizens should be consistent with the good news about the Messiah. Although these Christians in Philippi lived at the epicentre of Roman patriotism, their way of life was to be shaped by another king, Jesus. That might bring persecution, but they should not be afraid, because suffering for being associated with Jesus is a way of living out the story of Jesus himself. This eternal perspective enables their calling to live out their faith with boldness and conviction, even in the face of adversity.

5 Revelation, attitude and imitation

Philippians 2:1–16

The beautiful narrative of Philippians 2 offers us a number of profound insights into the nature of Christ's divinity. Paul makes a series of statements about Christ, his pre-existence and equality with God, his identification with humanity and his atoning act of sacrificial love. In 2:1–4, Paul tells the Philippians to be like-minded and united in purpose (*phronountes*, v. 2). He repeats the word and frames it in the context that they should think of themselves with modesty as Christ did (v. 5), literally translated, 'Have this attitude among yourselves which also in Christ Jesus.' Confusion about understanding this verse arises from the absence of the verb *is* in the second clause ('which also in Christ Jesus'). Did Paul intend for the reader to supply the same verb in this clause that appeared in the first clause ('Have this attitude among yourselves which *you also have* in Christ Jesus')? This is the view of those who adopt the kerygmatic interpretation, focusing on a personal encounter with Jesus. The proclamation of the gospel invites us to respond in faith, turning our lives towards God's redeeming love. According to this, the Philippians should have the attitude among themselves that is required of those who are 'in Christ' – that is, those who believe his death and resurrection. The listeners are urged to 'consider' others better than themselves 'in humility' (v. 3), as Jesus did, making himself of no reputation (vv. 5–7). Just as Christ did not 'consider' equality with God something to be exploited (v. 6) but 'humbled himself' (v. 8), Paul also refers to Christ's obedience (v. 8) when he speaks of the Philippians' obedience (v. 12).

If anything, having a mindset of obedience to God starts with thanksgiving and being grateful. Someone once said, 'I complained that I had no shoes until I met a man who had no feet.' One day, Christ's disciples started arguing about who would be the greatest in his kingdom. Jesus listened, then picked up a towel and a water basin and began washing their feet (John 13:1–10). When he finished, they were speechless, their hearts were exposed and their attitudes were corrected. 'Let this mind be in you which was also in Christ Jesus, who... made himself of no reputation' (v. 8). In essence: we serve as Christ does!

6 Witnessing to Christ's humility

Philippians 2:17–30

One of the most profound acts of humility conducted by Jesus was to wash the feet of his disciples (John 13:1–10). Such an extraordinary act of service demonstrated a love that goes beyond the usual parameters of expectations in order to put the needs of others first. The best way to express God's character, therefore, is through Christ's example of selfless sacrifice and obedience. Serving others becomes evidence of a willingness to put aside the innate need to be self-centred rather than God-focused. A heart orientation towards others goes against the human inclination towards selfishness and domination so often played out in society, from competitiveness to ostracising groups due to their race, class or gender. However, it's important to remember that God doesn't expect us to rely solely on our own efforts to do this. His power works within us to become more Christ-like in doing the Father's will. Living like Christ without the power of the Holy Spirit is fraught with difficulty in modern societies, where value is often attached to wealth, glamour, power, prestige and the accepted ways of doing things.

In Philippians 2:12, when Paul tells believers to 'work out their salvation', he is not asking them to work for their salvation on the final day. Instead, he advises them to conduct themselves in a manner worthy of the gospel of Christ while they wait for the final affirmation of their right standing before God on the day of Christ. They should focus on discerning what is best so that they can remain pure and blameless until the day of Christ. Timothy and Epaphroditus serve as faithful examples of the conduct that Paul has explicitly urged the Philippians to embody. Believers are to be united in spirit and live in humility and selflessness. In Timothy, Paul sees a genuine concern for the welfare of others, a willingness to put the needs of others before his own and a deep commitment to the things of Jesus Christ. Likewise, in Epaphroditus, Paul recognises loyalty and the dedication of a servant who is not only a brother in the faith but also a fellow worker and soldier in advancing the gospel. They are the kind of people who are living, breathing examples of the story of Jesus and they are worthy of invitation.

Guidelines

- Paul's perspective challenges us to rethink our life, death and priorities in the light of who Jesus is and what he has done. Rather than fearing death, we are encouraged to find hope in Christ's resurrection and live purposefully within a supportive faith community. As you read these verses, reflect on Christ's humility and how we, in turn, can demonstrate this to foster unity and show love. In what practical ways can we follow Christ's example of selflessness today?

- The joy Paul experiences when he sees the gospel advancing is not a superficial happiness that ignores the reality of affliction but a profound recognition of God's power to fulfil his plans, even in the face of human suffering. While believers should recognise and 'mourn' about suffering, as Paul mentions in another letter, they should not grieve as those with no hope (1 Thessalonians 4:13). This combination of hope and sorrow forms part of the Christian experience. How might you describe Paul's perspective on joy during these times?

- Paul discusses finding contentment in all circumstances, highlighting Christ as the ultimate sustainer over material possessions. How does Paul's emphasis on finding joy in every situation challenge societal norms prioritising material possessions?

- Humility is a significant theme in Philippians. How might we be aware of and avoid notions of false humility in our interactions with one another?

- Paul's letter to the Philippians highlights the need to rely on Christ for strength and sustenance so that we can flourish. What are the fundamental actions required for personal flourishing and spiritual growth? Why is it so challenging in a culture orientated towards consumerism?

- Individuals often seek explanations for suffering. Providing satisfactory answers to this question is challenging. How does Paul's assertion that suffering offers greater opportunity to know Christ align with this search for answers regarding the existence of suffering in the world?

1 Right belief as the foundation to righteous living

Philippians 3:1–16

The insistence on circumcision among early Jewish Christians was often raised by those who sought to cause trouble. These individuals believed, as Paul had done previously, that obedience to the Torah was a means of establishing righteousness before God. However, Paul's encounter with Jesus on the Damascus Road transformed his perspective (Acts 9:1–10). In a poignant demonstration of commitment and devotion, he recounts how since meeting the Lord he has willingly given up everything he once held dear, considering it all as 'filth' to participate in the sacrificial love and suffering of Jesus.

Paul also emphasises the importance of vigilance against those who seek to undermine faith. Being alert to those who are zealous in imposing their interpretation of God's grace on others encourages us to continually seek God's will for ourselves through prayer and scripture. Paul draws upon his experiences to illustrate the confidence of being securely held in Christ. While knowledge can encourage trust, combining expertise and experience solidifies one's determination.

Paul's encouragement to know Christ stems from his encounters with Christ and the transformative power that enables him to press forward towards a higher calling in Jesus Christ. This journey is marked by steady faith and a continuous pursuit of the divine purpose set before him.

In verse 9, Paul explains that God's response to human sin is the righteousness bestowed through faith in Christ. The term 'righteousness' used here communicates a judicial context, stemming from the classical Greek usage of the word to denote observance of customs, fairness, or what is deserved. The challenge arises when attempting to apply this traditional understanding directly to Paul's usage of the term, as it may lead to the misconception that 'the righteousness that comes from God' involves God compromising his righteousness as a judge and deeming us righteous through legal engineering, even when we are undeserving. God is good and just. The two are interlinked and go beyond our ordinary sense of justice. Our call is to seek God's righteousness and live out of it.

2 Where is your confidence?

Philippians 3:3–6

Paul's primary goal in writing is to inspire an unwavering trust in the Philippian believers by highlighting the freedom found in the gospel of Jesus' life, death and resurrection. The Philippian congregation had leaders who had misplaced their confidence in the law and who sought to undermine Paul's teachings by calling for strict adherence to Jewish customs as essential for a relationship with God. Specifically, they insisted on circumcision for the followers of Jesus, citing it as the hallmark of Jewish identity. However, Paul adamantly rejects this claim, asserting that his relationship with God, despite his circumcision, hinges entirely on Jesus rather than his Jewish heritage.

Before his encounter with Jesus, Paul shared these teachers' beliefs, methodically following the Old Testament laws as a model Hebrew. Despite having ample reason to pride himself on his Jewish heritage and religious observance, Paul now considers these aspects mere losses compared to the invaluable knowledge of Jesus. Everything else holds no value. He informs the Philippians that their relationship with God does not stem from adhering to laws but from trusting Jesus completely.

In laying out his qualifications, Paul recounts his strict adherence to the 613 laws of the Old Testament, which he once believed could earn God's favour. Now he emphasises that righteousness before God is not achieved through personal effort but through grace and faith in Jesus Christ, which is a gift from God. Christian hope does not lie in our goodness, what we have achieved or who we are, but in Jesus Christ, who welcomes sinners and offers healing, leading them into a relationship with God (1 Corinthians 12:19).

Due to the pervasiveness of sin, the human heart is naturally inclined to search for hope and confidence outside of Jesus Christ, whether that be in our identity, our religiosity or the good deeds we do to add to the work that Jesus accomplished. We can easily believe that if we live as good people, God will love and accept us, but this isn't the good news that Jesus taught. It is belief in the Lord Jesus Christ that is the hope of salvation (Acts 16:31), and nothing else! This is Paul's goal: to trust nothing but the good news of Jesus' life, death and resurrection.

3 God's confidence in all things

It's always a shock to hear about the fall from grace of someone we once had a high regard for. Whether it is a politician, Christian leader, friend or someone representing specific moral values, it is hard to understand how they could do something that is the opposite of the values they purported to hold. While it's good to follow the example of virtuous and ethical people, Jesus Christ is our primary, only truly reliable example. We may be tempted to rely on our own will and abilities for righteous living, but having accountability partners, senior church elders and supportive friends and family is healthy for our spiritual growth. In the text, we are reminded that we journey together as co-workers in the kingdom and citizens of heaven. Our task is to conform to the example set by Jesus, who submitted to the Father and died on the cross.

The section addressing Euodia and Syntyche stands out as a distinct appeal for reconciliation. Paul directly urges these individuals to resolve their conflict with each other. His language suggests that his main objective is to see them embody the qualities highlighted in earlier passages, such as having a Spirit-led fellowship marked by tenderness, compassion, mutual love and a shared sense of purpose. Their reconciliation is not expected to arise solely from human efforts but should be rooted in their unity 'in the Lord' (v. 4) This phrase signifies that their agreement should be inspired and empowered by the Lord, as seen elsewhere in the letter where a divine source guides human actions.

In 4:4–7, Paul emphasises four things: rejoicing, demonstrating gentleness, avoiding anxiety and presenting requests to God with thanksgiving The term 'gentleness' (*epieikeia*) conveys an attitude of kindness that contrasts with the expected reaction of retaliation in challenging circumstances. Because the Lord is at hand, the listeners are encouraged to be patient, generous and full of forbearance and restraint. While these instructions may initially appear unrelated, a deeper examination of the underlying meanings reveals a common thread that ties them together – the joy of the Lord. It is a joy that affirms, corrects and reminds us of where our confidence is located. In our modern context of culture wars and the encouragement of adversarial views, the children of God can provide a powerful witness that our confidence is founded not on ourselves or on our reputation, but in how we live out God's values and treat one another.

4 Loving from a place of peace

Philippians 3:17—4:7

'People will always need people' is a poem written by Benjamin Zephaniah to describe our social need for one another. Research has shown that well-being requires healthy sustained social connection. Any fractures in relationships are felt deeply, as our connectivity and sense of belonging and interconnection are part of our identity. Although some may enjoy their own company, human beings are naturally wired for relationships. Therefore, it can significantly affect us when we are not in relationship with others. Loving others is integral to following Jesus; after loving God, the second commandment is this: '"You shall love your neighbour as yourself." There is no other commandment greater than these' (Mark 12:31).

Paul is very clear how much he loves the community of Christians at Philippi and so is concerned about relationships that are not thriving. The epistle doesn't say much about Euodia and Syntyche, but it implies they need help in their relationship (4:2–3). They were Christians, but they didn't get along! We need to be honest about our relationships in order to have peace with God and one another. Therefore, we must talk to each other and address any difficulties we may experience at the earliest opportunity. This is part of loving others as ourselves. It begins with realising that we all require grace, forgiveness and the love of God. The peace of God passes all understanding, enabling deeper appreciation of another person, even though we may not understand them or be able to explain their behaviour towards us. But what we can do is rely on the Holy Spirit, who knows all things and guards our hearts and minds, bringing forth the fruit of kindness, gentleness and peace. Applying the principles outlined in Philippians 4:2–9, the passage addresses situations where theological principles like Christian unity are acknowledged in theory but lack practical application. It emphasises the value of fair and loving mediation and arbitration in resolving conflicts within the church. Supporting individuals to act as mediators and peacemakers within the church, in a similar fashion to Paul's address to Euodia and Syntyche, can help navigate disputes and promote unity. By heeding the guidance of prophetic voices and actively supporting efforts for reconciliation, the modern church can embody Paul's hope that believers would shine as beacons of light in a morally corrupt and distorted world.

5 Perseverance and satisfaction

Philippians 4:8–23

We use the word 'empowerment' to describe what feeling enabled or supported to do something might mean. It implies an authority or power which allows another to achieve things that would not usually happen without intervention. Throughout the letter to the Philippians, there is constant encouragement from Paul to understand from whom their strength, joy and hope comes. What's evident is a sense of worshipping God joyfully, irrespective of the circumstances. Moreover, Paul advises them not to worry or fret about anything, but to bring all concerns to God (4:6). Empowerment by the Holy Spirit means the peace of God allows us to come boldly to the throne of grace. How shall we continue to let go of those lurking fears? Philippians 4:8 answers with the attitude for us to adopt: 'Whatsoever things are true, whatsoever things are honest, whatsoever things are just, whatsoever things are pure, whatsoever things are lovely, whatsoever things are of good report… think on these things' (KJV).

Everything we choose, from the food we eat, to the tasks we complete, to the approach we adopt, has an element of choice. The psalmist was intentional each morning: 'This is the day the Lord has made, we will rejoice and be glad in it' (Psalm 118:24). One of the main themes in this last chapter of Philippians is the theme of contentment; not necessarily connected with personal circumstances but learned through union with and reliance on Christ (vv. 11–13). This does not mean divorcing oneself from current trials but rather a deepening of trust alongside an understanding of the spiritual importance of giving. We may often experience a sense of reluctance about what giving, not just out of our comfort but sacrificially, might mean for us. The irony is that when we do give, greed is rejected, together with the tendency to hoard, creating space for that very sense of contentment that Paul describes. In verses 10–23, Paul concludes with a heartfelt expression of gratitude to the Philippians for their generous gifts sent through Epaphroditus. This practical section holds theological significance, highlighting Paul's appreciation for their financial support while emphasising that his work is not dependent on this assistance. He also assures them that God will meet all their needs in return, not as compensation but as a gracious and freely given blessing. Giving freely out of love and obedience comes with a certainty that in God's wider economy, all will be provided for.

6 God's provision in all things

Philippians 4:8–23

On first reading about the nature of God's provision to Paul in verse 19, it is clear that this covers practical, spiritual and social needs – reflecting that the depth of God's generosity extends beyond material support to encompass provision to endure and persevere in all circumstances. Paul's gratitude towards the Philippians culminates in a doxology or hymn of praise to God that underscores the ultimate goal of his apostolic mission and the Philippians' partnership: the glory of God. While Paul acknowledges God's provision, his thanks capture again his gratitude for the way in which the Philippians have enabled that divine provision.

Through the example set by Paul and the Philippians in their detachment from material wealth, Christians are encouraged to guard themselves against the deceptive allure of wealth taking the place of God in their lives. Paul's contentment is rooted in the gospel's advancement, enabling him to find joy amid physical and emotional challenges. The Philippians' willingness to give demonstrates a similar detachment from material possessions, aligning with Paul's focus on the gospel's progress above all else. Ultimately, the support exchange between Paul and the Philippians reflects a shared commitment to advancing the gospel message, prioritising spiritual growth and service over material gain.

Neither rich nor poor are superior to one another, and both are encouraged to embrace the principle of giving for God's glory and the kingdom. This challenges the assertion that God is only focused on material wealth, the part of a prosperous kingdom. Standing in opposition to both prosperity theology and poverty theology, Pauline theology is underpinned by a sense of gratitude for the generosity of other believers and an appreciation of God's grace working through them. In the letter, there is no sense of flattery or manipulation, but a genuine desire to rejoice in the gifts of others and their generosity. In a modern context, where personal resources can be ostentatiously displayed, there is a need to examine and question the purpose of the things we acquire or the status we hold. Are they to dominate and promote a sense of envy, or are they to bless others and bring glory to God? Contentment comes from knowing the one who formed and shapes us and what our purpose is in accordance with his plan. That is when we have confidence that, irrespective of circumstances, God is our comfort and joy.

Guidelines

- Paul urged the congregation in Philippi to intervene in the conflict between Euodia and Syntyche, emphasising that division within the body of Christ weakens their collective testimony. How does Paul's call for intervention in conflicts within the church align with the importance of maintaining unity for the collective witness of the body of Christ today? What are the issues that require a courageous conversation among believers?

- Unity is crucial for the Christian community's well-being and faith-life together, especially in a context of persecution and challenging dialogues both within and outside. But at what cost should unity be achieved? Where should the lines be drawn?

- In the pursuit of unity, humility is necessary for fostering genuine empathy, connection and understanding among believers. What behaviours and attitudes contribute to establishing unity and meaningful relationships within your Christian community, especially in the face of the differing experiences of hardship or social challenges that people may have?

- Paul's instruction to think about commendable things suggests focusing on positive, virtuous and pure qualities in the world, in one's thoughts and in one's actions. Often, these are not only found in the church but also in wider creation. What challenges might such positive, righteous and pure attributes hold in fostering healthy attitudes and actions in individual believers and the church as a whole?

Prayer in an age of neoliberalism

Valerie Hobbs

What does it mean to be religious in an age of neoliberalism? This question was posed a few years ago to Jewish scholar Dr Susannah Heschel. In response, Dr Heschel lamented that few in her faith are now taught how to pray, how to think about God, how to cultivate a sense of God's presence. The self is now, in neoliberal terms, an 'entrepreneurial project', an object of one's own will and endeavours.

Without critical care and attention, our prayers follow suit, functioning as an attempt to bend God's will to the individual's, to incline God's ear my way. 'God, here is my laundry list of things I need an answer to, my to-do list.' God's name is too often evoked to baptise our own self-reliance, our own decisions, to sacralise our plans with the power of God's authority. If things then happen as I see fit, God must have blessed it. And if we as individuals haven't been 'blessed' in the ways we've asked, as our society honours – if we are still poor, still declining in mental and physical health, still jobless, still unhoused – well, then, we haven't prayed hard enough, long enough. After all, God helps those who help themselves.

As one antidote to the effects of neoliberalism in Christian prayer, this set of notes works through several themes of Old Testament prayers: God's name, God's everlasting love, God's care and comfort, God's memory and God's zeal for the purity of his house. These aim to recentre our prayers on seeking God's face, his very person, asking for the intimacy of God's presence in our lives through Jesus Christ by the Spirit, and through this, a peace resting in his divine will that passes all understanding.

Unless otherwise stated, Bible quotations are taken from NIV.

1 Asking God to be God: the lifeblood of prayer

Genesis 4

The second half of Genesis 4:26 is widely understood to include the Bible's first reference to prayer. But its meaning is ambiguous.

Translators have made of this what they will, some rendering the verse to mark the arrival of faithful worship, even preaching. Others see here the hope of prayer, later fulfilled in part when Abram builds an altar and calls upon the Lord's name. Still others interpret this passage as announcing the spread of idolatry, following rabbinical tradition, i.e. 'At that time, profaning the name of the Lord began' (ISV).

This more literal translation is perhaps truest to all this complexity: 'Then it was begun to call upon the name of the Lord.' After all, by now, Genesis has recorded not only the cultivation of life but also another prolific theme: murder, revenge and blood guilt.

In chapter 4, the writer amplifies these oppositions, starting with Abel, earth's first recorded shepherd. Abel's name also carries a message, meaning 'vapour' or 'breath', a life force again gifted by God, then promptly suffocated by Cain. Abel's blood seeps into the earth's mouth, bars earth's strength from Cain. Indeed, the very voice of Abel's blood cries out to God. Perhaps this lament for justice is, in truth, the first prayer.

This tension carries on painfully in Cain's retreat eastward, symbolising wandering and unrest and the construction of the first recorded city. From Cain comes also Tubal-Cain, forger of metals, father of weapons, and Lamech, with his own 'divinely competitive song of vengeance' (Thompson, 2011). And yet, positioned against all this absurd frontiersmanship is the cheering advent of Seth the substitute and of Enosh.

And so now, through somewhat dizzied vision, we spy in Genesis 4:26 this reference to prayer and therein the announcement of two houses. The first involves a perversion of God's name, a premonition of Babel, erected by men seeking a name for themselves, a den of thieves. The second is its counterpart, God's house of prayer, occupied by those who long for the name of God, whose essence is to be himself and to do what he will do.

Our Father of Abel and of Abraham, through Jesus we cry out from the dust of this unjust earth. We call upon your name. We ask you to be who you are.

2 Naming God in prayer

Quite rightly, Hagar has received attention as the first human in the Bible to name God: El Roi, Living-One-Who-Sees. Hundreds of years later, another woman near water, another figure from the margins of God's house, likewise calls on the name of the Lord. 'Messiah,' she says, prompting Jesus' answer: 'I, the one speaking to you – I am he' (John 4:7–26).

As yesterday's notes explored, in calling upon the name of God, these two women perform a powerful prayer, signalling their recognition of God's essence and his will. Where God names and renames various people in the biblical story to signal a shift in their identity and purpose, God is never nameless, nor does his name ever change. Rather, the name of God becomes visible to those whose eyes the Spirit opens to God's person, character and works.

In Hagar's case, it is the words of the angel of the Lord which illuminate for her the name of God. His divine speech echoes the promise God had only recently made to Hagar's master, constituting a pivotal moment in biblical history, when God promises Abram a son. Now, the angel extends this same covenant to a victim of oppression, mother of many and of Ishmael, a wild donkey of a man; a symbol of those who are unsettled, anxious, in exile, lost.

And many years later, we meet the anti-type, Saul, who searched without success for his father's own lost donkeys (1 Samuel 9:3). And even later, God, having heard the prayers of the women who name him, reveals the astounding scope of his vision, stretching as far as wherever all the lost ones roam, even the wildest of donkeys. Our God-Who-Lives-and-Sees tells his disciples of the place, and off they go (Mark 11:2).

Living-God-Who-Sees, we pray for all who are unsettled, anxious and lost. Only you know where they are. You alone can find them. Teach us how to love them.

3 Prayer for the marriage of the Lamb

Genesis 24

The prayers in verses 12–14 by the most elderly and high ranking of Abraham's servants further illuminate several themes already developing across the earliest prayers of the Old Testament. First, we see that this senior servant names God, calling him then to be who he is and to do what he does. Given humanity's everlasting eagerness to turn our prayers towards our own plans and our own power, we surely need these constant reminders. Recall that in verse 7, Abraham has told this servant what to expect of God, based on God's own covenant promise to him.

Next, we note the theme of water, which represents both judgement and salvation across the biblical text. By this time, Abraham and his house have settled in the region of the Negev, to whose edge he had first journeyed after God first called him. The Negev is a place of extreme beauty, wild with desert but likewise with springs of water, of life, of joy, of love. Moses later sends twelve spies to scope out this same land of promise; it's also the place which Achsah, daughter of Caleb, riding on a donkey, would later request as a wedding gift. 'Give me a blessing,' Achsah says. 'Since you have given me land in the Negev, give me also springs of water' (Judges 1:15).

Abraham's servant's request for physical refreshment is later echoed and extended in Jesus' encounter with the Samaritan woman at the well. There, our Messiah reveals the meaning of the servant's prayer for Rebekah in all its fullness, that by the name that is Jesus, through the water of the Spirit, we who are appointed for the marriage of the Lamb shall never thirst, even to eternal life.

God of Eternal Refreshment, we believe your promise to be with us wherever we go. We are your treasured possession. Guide us in the way of your will.

4 Prayer in the shadows

One of the most enigmatic of the Bible's shadow stories is in this chapter, where Hezekiah, king of Judah, is about to die. The prophet Isaiah comes to deliver the bad news, and the text says that Hezekiah turns his face to the wall to pray for God to remember him and his good deeds. As he prays, Hezekiah weeps bitterly.

In response, before Isaiah has left the middle court, the place of burnt offerings, God declares he has heard Hezekiah's prayer in secret. Hezekiah will be healed, and on the third day he will go up to the house of the Lord. Isaiah next directs the king's attendants to take a cake of figs, that fruit whose leaves Adam and Eve used to conceal their shame, and to cover Hezekiah's mortal wound, a blistering boil. These are powerful pictures! And immediately, Hezekiah recovers and asks for a further sign. Isaiah obliges, offering him God's power over the shadow of passing time. Hezekiah answers, and the shadow is driven back, presumably not by the sun, symbol of Baal as it was, but by the supernatural radiance of the Shekinah Glory, the appearance of God himself.

In all this, God shows us what Hezekiah knew as he lay dying and prayed desperately; that our days lengthen as a shadow descending the stairs. Our hope through prayer echoes his own, our cry to the same mightier King of Judah. Our Messiah guides his people through the valley of the shadow of death. He calls us into the shade of God's hand, under the shelter of his wings. And there we wait, until the Father completes in full his sign for Hezekiah, until the shadows flee away. Our God holds us until the destruction of sickness, death and judgement passes by. We sing for joy, for he has been our help, our Father of lights, with whom there is no variation or shifting shadow.

Father of Light, remember now that through Jesus' good deeds we have walked before you in truth, by your Spirit. Bring the glory of your peace to us in the shadows, on earth as in heaven.

5 Prayer for remembrance

In Old Testament times, the cupbearer to the king embodied extraordinary responsibility. The cupbearer served wine to the king, but he also tasted the wine before the king drank, for quality and poison: a risky office of oppositions.

Cupbearers of note include the man Joseph meets, thrown into prison for offending Egypt's ruler. While there, the cupbearer has an enigmatic dream, which Joseph interprets; the cupbearer will live. In exchange for this interpretation, Joseph asks the cupbearer to intercede for him with Pharaoh, but the cupbearer forgets. Until later, when Pharaoh too is plagued by strange dreams and the cupbearer suddenly recalls his promise.

The memory of our second cupbearer, Nehemiah, does not stumble. As Nehemiah takes up the wine and gives it to King Artaxerxes, so he also takes up the case of God's people, pleading with the king to send him 'to the city of my fathers' tombs' (NKJV), that he might rebuild it. Nehemiah's story further intertwines the cupbearer vocation and its meanings: life and death; memory and forgetfulness.

The book of Nehemiah records multiple prayers of memory, stirring the people's failing recollection of their mighty God, asking God to remember the word to Moses, to remember Nehemiah and to remember too those who had tried to frighten God's people, those who defiled the priesthood and the covenant. God's memory, like the wine the cupbearer carries, both saves and condemns. Here is Eden's life-and-death duality, the cup of the Lord and the cup of demons. In that first garden, Adam and Eve chose the latter, and such is our sad inheritance.

But who has taken out of our hand the cup of reeling, the chalice of anger? Who has drunk it, even to its dregs? Who contends for his people before the King, ruler of heaven and earth, proclaiming, 'You will never drink it again' (Isaiah 51:21–23)? As the soldiers gather to arrest Jesus, our champion cupbearer of unfailing memory, mortification and mettle intermingle in his words: 'Put your sword into the sheath. Shall I not drink the cup which My Father has given Me?' (John 18:11, NKJV).

Lord over Life and Death, you promise to remove the cup of wrath from us forever. When our eyes see only our own weakness, when empire builders threaten your house, remember us. Keep us from violence, our feet in the path of peace.

6 Prayer for consuming zeal

The book of Nehemiah is so compelling, so piercing, so full of love and longing for God, so full of Christ. Nehemiah rebuilds the temple after exile, as Jesus would rebuild the temple of his body, even us. But there's more.

As chapter 13 begins, Nehemiah is away from Jerusalem. While he's gone, the people of God turn again to evil, even preparing a room in the temple courts for regional Persian governor and troublemaker Tobiah, for his own uses. When Nehemiah returns and sees all this corruption, his heart burns with eagerness for God's purposes. 'Remember me, O my God,' he prays, 'for good' (NKJV).

Nehemiah's prayerful commitment to the purity of God's house brings the life and ministry of Jesus Christ into focus. Where Nehemiah expels Tobiah from the temple, restores the tithes to the Levites and the sacred singers, contends with marriages leading to sin and reinstates the sabbath, Jesus too goes up to Jerusalem and finds in the temple those selling oxen, sheep and doves, and the money-changers seated at their tables. And having made a scourge of cords, Jesus drove them all out of the temple, poured out the money and overturned their tables. Where Nehemiah, following Abraham, arranges for the supply of wood for sacrifice and for the first fruits, by Jesus' death on a wooden cross, by his resurrection, Christ has purified us from all our sins, he the first fruits of those who are asleep.

What Nehemiah had begun, Jesus perfected, so that all present would understand how his blood cleanses our conscience of dead works, trains our eyes for heaven and equips us for glory. The watching disciples remembered what was written by King David and on Nehemiah's heart too, that zeal for God's house would be all-consuming (Psalm 69:9; John 2:17). There is now no wrath against those God loves, his people called by his name. By the Spirit, we are born again through the living and enduring word of God, now the first fruits among God's creatures.

And what is to be our response to our Saviour's zeal for us, his own body, his house of prayer?

Remember us, our God, for good. Where there is injustice, where we fail to love kindness, where humility is lacking, Lord, purify your house.

Guidelines

Like all the practices of our faith, our prayer takes place in a context of immense pressure to work harder, be more productive, to achieve, to be fitter, happier, healthier, wealthier, to make a name for oneself – to fix all that is broken. But membership in God's house of prayer involves meditation not on the empires of earth but on the essence, promises and works of God; God's kingdom come, God's will be done. After Job, even in our desperate laments from the shadows, Christian prayer in earthly exile seeks first the beatific vision, the Shekinah Glory of God in the face of Jesus Christ.

Dr Susannah Heschel tells a story of her father's namesake, a Hasidic spiritual nurturer called Abraham Joshua Heschel. When asked how anyone could possibly pray for so many people, so many problems, Rebbe Heschel replied:

'When someone comes to me and they pour out their troubles, I open my heart, and their sorrows come into my heart and make a scar. When I go to pray, I open my heart to God and I say, "Look at all these scars."'

Prayer is a powerful act of faith in who God is and in his perfect memory. We need only draw near to him and see what he will do.

FURTHER READING

Faith & Leadership (2015) 'What does it mean to be religious in an age of neoliberalism?' Available at: **parliamentofreligions.org/articles/what-does-it-mean-to-be-religious-in-an-age-of-neoliberalism**.

Thomas L. Thompson, 'Genesis 4 and the Pentateuch's reiterative discourse: some Samaritan themes' in József Zsengellér (ed), *Samaria, Samarians, Samaritans: Studies on Bible, history and linguistics* (Dr Gruyter, 2011), pp. 9–22.

Finding faith and challenging culture

Victoria Omotoso

One of my favourite chapters in the Bible is John 17, which never fails to bring tears to my eyes. Here Jesus prays first for the work he was sent to do and the unshakeable relationship between himself and his Father. Then he prays for his disciples, who have walked with him, prayed with him, listened to him, cried and laughed with him every day for the past three and a half years. He prays for their unity, their mission and their protection. Finally, he prays for all future believers, for their unity and that love reigns.

They say, 'The apple doesn't fall far from the tree.' As far as genetics go, we tend to take on the mannerisms or characteristics of our parents. We involuntarily inherit part of who they are. When we invite Jesus into our lives, we are known to be children of God: manifesting his characteristics and aiming to follow his example.

The call to be God's children involves recognising our place in the world we live in. The apostle Peter identifies us as 'foreigners' in this world, as exiles who are often despised (1 Peter 2:11-12). Yet we are called to walk in love, to remain cordial and neighbourly. We see this in Daniel, who knows in whom his identity lies, although he faces strong opposition.

John 17 offers profound insight into the heart of our Saviour and his concern for those he calls his own. Jesus knows the challenges we face as believers in a world that is often resistant to God. Yet he does not pray for his disciples to be out of the world, although he knows they are like 'a fish out of water' in that they do not belong here, just as he did not belong. Instead, he asks for them to be kept safe, secure, united and holy (vv. 15-16).

Unless otherwise stated, Bible quotations are taken from the NLT.

1 No compromise

Daniel 1:1-17

Living in a culture that is often at odds with your faith is not a new phenomenon. The Bible gives us examples of heroes of faith who have walked this path before us, and one such hero is Daniel. The story of Daniel begins with the invasion of Judah by King Nebuchadnezzar in 586BC. This invasion led to the destruction of the temple in Jerusalem, the capture of Judah's royal families and the loss of Judah's independence. In Babylon, Daniel and his friends, Hananiah, Mishael and Azariah, found themselves in the king's palace, expected to share in the king's food and wine.

Living in Babylon brought exposure to a different culture, a different language, a different way of living that challenged all the ways of God that Daniel and his friends had known. The consequences of captivity were first, separation from both their geographical culture and their religious culture. They were now vulnerable to new influences. Second, they were eunuchs, with no hope of a lineage or legacy; and third, they were being actively taught the ways of the Babylonians.

Yet within this environment Daniel did not compromise his faith. As Christians, we cannot detach ourselves from the culture we find ourselves in. Nevertheless, we can make a conscious decision 'not to defile' ourselves (v. 8). In Babylon, the description of Daniel and his friends' choice not to 'defile themselves' with the food of the king indicates that the food had been sacrificed to idols. To partake in the consumption of this food would be tacitly to accept the authority of idols, to affiliate with a false religion. Countercultural living required a stand of faith.

Despite Daniel's uncompromising stance, it did not undermine the excellence of his service, work and duty to the king and the palace. Daniel also sought permission to go against the ways of Babylon. He was respectful; not seeking out offence. As children of God, in our strange environment, we are called to continue in a state of 'doing good' and be in submission to human authority as part of our service to honour God (1 Peter 2:12-13). It is a tightrope to be respectful (v. 17) and uncompromising at the same time, yet, for the sake of the Lord, it is the nucleus of how we navigate this world.

2 Ready, steady, stand!

A saying often attributed to Alexander Hamilton, one of the founding fathers of the United States of America, is: 'If you stand for nothing, you'll fall for everything.' Brought into exile in the kingdom of Babylon, Daniel learned the language, studied the literature and even acquired a Babylonian name, Belshazzar. He worked as one of the wise men, which meant he had to fully understand the customs and immerse himself in the culture. Yet he stood firm in his faith and did not compromise his integrity.

In chapter 6, years on from his first arrival in Babylon, this integrity was challenged by a decree that everyone had to bow down to the king for 30 days. Verse 10 tells us, 'But when Daniel learned that the law had been signed, he went home and knelt down as usual in his upstairs room, with its windows open toward Jerusalem. He prayed three times a day, just as he had always done, giving thanks to his God.' He could have compromised; after all, the requirement was only for 30 days. Yet Daniel continued to pray, knowing full well the possible consequences of his actions.

In Matthew's gospel, Jesus highlights the cost to pay if we are truly in line with following the way of God. The Amplified Bible emphasises this: 'Then Jesus said to His disciples, "If anyone wishes to follow Me [as My disciple], he must deny himself [set aside selfish interests], and take up his cross [expressing a willingness to endure whatever may come] and follow Me [believing in Me, conforming to My example in living and, if need be, suffering or perhaps dying because of faith in Me]"' (Matthew 16:24). The world will only respond when it sees us as Christians living in a state of self-sacrifice; submitting our will and inclinations and practising the process of giving, rather than attempting to dictate or assume a sense of superiority. Daniel's greatest stand was his quiet spirit in his regular commitment to God; he had given up all aspects of self-preservation to be fully and wholly God's servant. What are we willing to give up or let go to follow Jesus faithfully?

3 The identity trap

Matthew 16:21-28; 1 Peter 2:1-8

Following Jesus involves the denial of self: becoming more willing to put down our own will, desires and pleasures, and to honour Christ in our everyday living. It does not mean that we lose our individuality but rather we recognise that our true identity is found solely in Jesus.

The act of following Jesus entails the taking up of one's cross (Matthew 16:24). The idea of the cross comes from the Greek word *stauros*, which literally means 'an upright stake'. Figuratively, it refers to the sacrifice that each believer makes. A cross, in whatever way it presents itself - a physical or mental illness, a failed or difficult relationship, a form of addiction - always leaves a door open for our full dependency on Jesus. *Stauros* in turn derives from the word *histemi*, which means to make a stand. The paradox is that as we take up our cross, we are also standing.

Many people are willing to accept Jesus as their Saviour but often less willing to accept Jesus as Lord. The term 'Lord' is derived from the Hebrew, *Adonai*, 'the owner'. Making Jesus our owner goes against the dominant zeitgeist of today. So much of our cultural rhetoric revolves around the idea of 'being in charge of your own destiny' and 'being the captain of your own ship'. Yet our true identity is found in Jesus alone; our ships should be captained by Jesus.

In 1 Peter 2, the apostle writes to churches scattered throughout the empire, addressing the persecuted church living as 'exiles', 'foreigners' in a culture that opposed the way of Christ (1 Peter 1:11). Peter reminds them who they are in Christ and what their identity means in their daily living. In verse 5, he states: 'And you are living stones that God is building into his spiritual temple. What's more, you are his holy priests. Through the mediation of Jesus Christ, you offer spiritual sacrifices that please God.' First, we are called to be living stones, part of God's temple building, founded upon Jesus Christ the cornerstone (v. 6). When we recognise that our identity is rooted in Jesus, then we can live intentionally in the will of God. Practically, this means being in a state of surrender, where even our very essence is found in Christ alone.

4 Holy, holy, holy!

Deuteronomy 14:1-7; 1 Peter 2:9-10

I once heard a saying that Christians should be like dolphins and not jellyfish. Dolphins swim against the ocean's current, while jellyfish swim with the current whichever direction it flows. This concept harks back to Jesus' words in John 17 that although we are in the world, we 'do not belong to the world' (v. 14). In Deuteronomy 14, the laws that are given to the Israelites demonstrate their call to be holy and separate from the surrounding cultures: a reminder for God's children that there are specific expectations to adhere to. The opening address, 'Since you are the people of the Lord', emphasises that everything in the instructions to follow is directly related to the fact of their belonging to God.

Often, the idea of holiness is seen as something that is restrictive or limiting. However, holiness simply means to be distinct and separate. In the Old Testament, God reveals himself as *El Hakkadosh*, the holy God. Consequently, God commands the people of Israel to be holy, which is to be physically manifested through the act of circumcision and the separation of certain permissible animals for consumption. This process served to separate the Israelites from the surrounding nations. God separates himself from all other gods; he is distinct and different. Deuteronomy 10:17 exclaims: 'For the Lord your God is God of gods and Lord of lords. He is the great God, mighty and awesome God.' These words should be at the heart of how we live, 'You must be holy because I, the Lord your God, am holy' (Leviticus 19:1), in accordance with our identity as God's people.

Peter reaffirms this notion of holiness by reminding the scattered and persecuted Christians that they too are called to be holy, to be separate, to be distinct from the culture. As Christians today, we still receive this call to be a holy people; individuals who form a collective culture in which God reigns. The idea of possession or ownership is demonstrated in the recipients of the apostle's letter being addressed as 'God's chosen people', won through the grace of Jesus Christ (1 Peter 1:1). It is a sign that we are in the ocean, but swimming against the natural flow of the current. When we attend to the call of being God's holy priests, his chosen people, his holy nation, we begin to manifest this practically in our actions and interactions with others.

5 Stranger, no danger

1 Peter 2:11-21

If you have ever travelled to a foreign country, you will know what it feels like to be a stranger. Everything is new and unfamiliar; you hear new sounds, smell new smells, see new sights. While you may enjoy the experience and appreciate the kindness of the people, you are constantly reminded of the fact that you are still a stranger; you are not at home. Although you may love the hotel and the escape from the monotony of the everyday, at some point you will find yourself saying, 'There's no place like home.'

There are many parallels between the experiences of Daniel and the believers of 1 Peter. Themes such as persecution, suffering, remaining faithful to God and trusting God are constant motifs. However, one of the most prominent of these is the idea of living as foreigners or strangers in the world. Part of embracing a countercultural lifestyle is recognising that we are indeed strangers in this world. Being strangers *in* the world does not mean that we should be strangers *to* the world; rather, it means that in our distinctiveness we should be a witness to and a light for Jesus. The word used here in the Greek refers to being a pilgrim: not a pilgrim in a state of journeying but one in a state of residency, as one who resides in a foreign country.

While we are still in the world, we live with our eyes fixed on Jesus and on the goal of eternal life with him. In 1 Peter 2:11, the apostle acknowledges the constant warfare that our status as strangers brings: 'Dear friends, I warn you as "temporary residents and foreigners" to keep away from worldly desires that wage war against your very souls.' In a war, one party seeks domination over another; here, worldly desires are in constant opposition to the ways of Christ. Things that used to entertain us are now unfamiliar or no longer appeal; jokes or language that we were accustomed to now sound a siren in our ears. The ways of the world are now strange to us because we are ultimately citizens of heaven.

6 Reconciliation

John 13:31-35; 1 John 3:1-18

There is something poignant and precious about a person's final words. As with the final words of Jacob to his sons, or the last words of David to Solomon, at the last supper Jesus begins to give his final messages to his disciples. During these last days of his earthly ministry, the tension among his disciples was mounting and it was becoming increasingly difficult to be a follower of Jesus. There were intense emotions of confusion, uncertainty and possibly strife, overshadowed by the knowledge that someone, one of their very own, would betray their leader. In the midst of this turbulence, Jesus shares with them, 'So now I am giving you a new commandment: Love each other. Just as I have loved you, you should love each other. Your love for one another will prove to the world that you are my disciples' (vv. 34-35).

Showing love to each other was a distinctive mark to prove discipleship. Being a disciple of Christ requires one not just to follow Christ but to imitate Christ in words and deeds. Discipleship is a lifestyle rooted in the love of Christ, requiring true disciples to demonstrate that love even in a world that may not reciprocate it. To belong to Christ means that, just like Christ, our presence and witness in the world may be met with hatred (1 John 3:13). The Greek word used here for 'hate' is *μισεῖ (misei)*, which translates as 'to detest' or 'think of with less esteem'. Instead of simply associating the word with hatred, as we may think, it conveys the idea that, as Christians, we are often despised or held in low esteem compared to others. However, despite this, Christ instructs us to persist in a life of love. The hallmark of countercultural living, taught to those scattered believers of the early church, is to persist in love and even respond with a blessing when people insult you! The way of the world often prioritises that we get the upper hand. But the way of Christ teaches us to be humble and meek: a clear sign that the life we live in Christ is no longer our own.

Guidelines

A friend who identified as a Christian was faced with the task of planning a Halloween work party, despite not celebrating Halloween. She was initially reluctant to do it, but was encouraged by her church Bible study group to proceed, so that by successfully organising the party, she could demonstrate her good work ethic and thus serve as an effective witness for Christ to her co-workers. Is this something you would do?

As 'foreigners' in this world, how does your work, your ministry or your faith community serve as your witness to Christ? In what ways can we truly beam Christ's love into the world without being part of the world? Perhaps, in the coming week, you can keep note of the conversations you have and be more conscious of your reactions and responses, seeking out new opportunities to be a witness of Christ's love.

FURTHER READING

St Augustine of Hippo, *The City of God* (Hendrickson Publishers, 2009).

Timothy Keller, *Every Good Endeavor: Connecting your work to God's work* (Viking, 2012).

H. Richard Nicbuhr, *Christ and Culture* (Harper & Row, 1975).

Leviticus: holy living and holy dying

Peter Hatton

In the next two weeks we shall be exploring a book which, for many Christians, has become a byword for difficulty and irrelevance. As the Revd Timothy Lovejoy, pastor in *The Simpsons*, affirms of scripture, 'it's all good', so we shouldn't have 'favourites'. However, I have loved Leviticus ever since I first read it as a new convert to Christianity many years ago.

Why? What on earth is the attraction of a book that spends its first seven chapters describing the details of obscure sacrificial rites, which, since the destruction of the Jerusalem temple by the Romans in AD70, cannot even be performed; that devotes a whole chapter (Leviticus 18) to sexual practices described as 'abominations'; that approves, or, at least, describes without disapproval, several acts of violence, divine and human.

Perhaps I am rather peculiar in being drawn to challenging texts that seem, at first sight, impenetrable. Writings such as Leviticus deconstruct our naive tendency to think that contemporary culture is somehow 'normal', indeed 'normative'. We must not forget that the vast majority of the world's population today are not *WEIRD* (Western Educated Industrialised Rich Democratic). For many outside our narrow confines, the world of Leviticus is not a distant, remote one. For instance, in much of the world, the eating of meat is infrequent, and its source is not hidden in production-line slaughterhouses; the taking of an animal's life in the context of ritual and worship is what people expect and value.

The challenge of Leviticus to contemporary western Christians, is, if my own experience is any guide, even more radical. We find it, I think, increasingly difficult to be 'countercultural'; to enter a space in which we can discern and reject powerful, idolatrous forces trying to make us conform to their ungodly worldview. Leviticus' central concern is to promote that distancing from corrupt cultural norms, which scripture calls 'holiness'. May reading it in the next fortnight encourage us to seek 'that holiness without which no one will see the Lord' (Hebrews 12:14, NRSV).

1 All for Jesus

Leviticus 1

Sacrifices were at the heart of all worship of the gods in antiquity. Indeed, among the ancient Greeks, the nearest expression to our word 'religion' was *hoi thusioi* ('the sacrifices'). A religion without sacrifices would have been beyond strange; almost unimaginable. We can see, then, that God, seeking to communicate with his people, would choose to accommodate himself to their existing worldview by permitting sacrificial rites to honour him.

However, the first chapter of Leviticus describes some surprising, counter-cultural aspects in the most important offering made to YHWH, ('the Lord'). This is the 'burnt-offering' (Hebrew *ōlāh*, literally 'that which goes up'), first mentioned in verse three. This describes the way that the whole animal, after it has been slaughtered and prepared (except for its hide which is given to the priests), is burnt on the altar, and so 'goes up' as a 'pleasing aroma' to *YHWH*.

'What a waste!' we might say. Most ancient people would have agreed. The normal practice was for certain choice portions of a sacrificed animal to be laid before the idol of a god. A screen would be placed round the idol and its 'meal', and, after a decent interval in which the god would eat what they needed to, this meat would be distributed among the priests. The other meat would be eaten by the worshippers, and any surplus sold in the markets. In this way of thinking, the gods are, in a strange way, dependent on their worshippers for food.

Psalm 50:12–13 explicitly denies that Israel's God needs us to satisfy his hunger. The same understanding is implicit in this chapter. What makes a sacrifice acceptable to YHWH and what opens up a way for sinful humans into his holy presence (the point of the 'atonement' language in verse four) is the costly obedience that such offerings demonstrate. An *ōlāh* is not an attempt to win divine favour; nor does God need it; but he delights in a willingness to give freely and without any expectation of return.

The father of someone I knew in my youth found his son's decision to give up a very well-paid job in finance to become a pastor perplexing. 'What a waste!' was his judgement. God, however, was, I believe, pleased by this 'fragrant offering'.

2 Party time!

Given the space available we won't be able to comment fully on every section of Leviticus and so we skip over chapter two. However, if you can, do read its instructions for the grain offerings. Since a small part of these were burnt as offerings to YHWH, but most of the grain was eaten by the priests, they prepare us for the peace offerings (Hebrew *shelamîm*, connected to the word *shalom*, 'peace') of Leviticus chapter three. We might not realise it from chapter three, but Leviticus 7:11–18 makes it clear that while some of the offering, especially the fat, was burnt, and another portion was given to the priests, most of the meat was returned to the worshippers for their own consumption.

There are many puzzling details here. While the prohibition on consuming blood is well known – and connected with the understanding that blood contains and represents an animal's life, which belongs to God – why should fat be burnt rather than eaten? We are not told; as we are not told so much about the background of this and other rites in Leviticus. We should remember that the book functions in part as a 'hands-on' instruction manual for priests, rather than a theological treatise.

However, these obscurities should not distract from the central insight, namely that here the worshippers are commanded to feast and celebrate as they consume a rich feast of animal protein, a rare and joyful occasion in this poor, undernourished society. The command in 7:15–18 that the meat should be eaten on the same day as the sacrifice or, at the latest, on the day after (depending on the motive behind the offering) meant that the number feasting would have been large, not restricted to the worshipper and his family. They might even have had to invite complete strangers to ensure everything would be consumed.

Before the holy meal in which we remember the sacrificial death of Jesus, there is, in many churches, an opportunity to exchange a sign of peace. This need not be a formality. Is there someone in your fellowship with whom you do not feel at peace? Why not use the next Communion to put that right? And/or you could invite them over for supper!

3 Ignorance is no excuse

Leviticus 5:14–19

This reading insists that even when we get things wrong without meaning to, or even knowing that we are doing wrong, costly atonement is still necessary. In fact, this section repeats and summarises the teaching of the previous two chapters which deal with unintentional wrongdoing of all sorts, including unknowingly offending in 'ritual matters' ('the holy things of YHWH'). This seems harsh and unfair. Surely being ignorant that we are doing anything wrong should excuse us?

We might admit that people can choose to ignore sin when it is convenient to do so. We are quick to condemn the wilful ignorance of many concerning the evils of the transatlantic slave trade. We are slower to ask where the moral blind spots are for us today. However, surely getting mere ritual matters unintentionally wrong cannot be so serious?

Ancient Israel's understanding of God forbade such a relaxed attitude. Although YHWH's loving kindness and goodness were undoubted, there was also a deep sense of his immense power and his unpredictable 'otherness'. The primary purpose of ritual was to enable his people to enter his awesome presence safely; so it had to be done right. When it was done wrong, as, for instance, when the ark of the covenant was brought up to Jerusalem in the wrong way, by the wrong people, and when a non-Levite, Uzzah, with all the best intentions, touched the holy dwelling place of YHWH, then the consequences were disastrous (see 2 Samuel 6:1–10). A modern parallel might be the intentional, alert care needed when approaching a working nuclear reactor.

Arguably these chapters bespeak a better attitude to God and the things of God than the casual, even complacent, over-familiarity of some modern Christians! The incarnation of God in Jesus should not encourage us to think we can patronise God or coopt him into our little schemes. Rather, it should increase our awe and wonder.

When Mr Beaver reveals to the puzzled children in *The Lion, the Witch and the Wardrobe* that the rightful ruler of Narnia is Aslan, a lion, Susan asks if he is 'quite safe'. 'Safe?' responds Beaver indignantly. ''Course he isn't safe. But he's good. He's the king, I tell you.'

4 The support staff

If, with some caution, we take the analogy between God and a reactor further, then Israel's priests, whose duties meant that they often approached his awe-inspiring presence, had to be especially protected, just as do workers in the nuclear industry. So, the complex rituals in which Aaron and his sons are 'consecrated', 'clothed' and ordained are intended to ensure that they are not just equipped, but also protected, in their ministry. In Leviticus 10, when two of Aaron's sons offer 'unholy fire', unsanctioned by YHWH, 'fire came out from the presence of the Lord and consumed them, and they died before the Lord' (Leviticus 10:1–2). Quite why this fire was so 'unholy' (or 'strange' – was there some idolatrous rite involved?) is unclear, but the incident underlines the dangers that face Aaron and his sons as they minister in the holy presence. We might wonder why anyone would willingly agree to serve in this way!

Were Israel's priests especially privileged? Not compared to those who served idols. Ancient temples were powerful institutions whose elite priesthood enjoyed wealth, privilege and political power. They were major landowners and, because their solid buildings offered security, they functioned as banks, lending silver deposited with them at great profit.

In contrast, Aaron and his sons are part of the tribe of Levi, forbidden from holding land and subsisting mainly from a tithe levied on the other, landed tribes. Indeed, in Leviticus where there is, as yet, no temple building, and ministry is conducted in the 'tent of meeting', the priests share the vulnerable, nomadic existence of their fellows. Of course, their role as those who made Israel's worship possible and drew near to God in the holy places, earned faithful priests gratitude and respect from their fellow Israelites. However, in comparison with other ancient priests, the 'sons of Aaron' had little by way of status and advantage. The greatest benefit they enjoyed was the joy that comes from serving God and others.

Further caution is advisable when comparing the 'Aaronic' priests with those set aside for Christian ministry, who don't belong to a particular 'tribe' within God's people, but offer that oversight without which its priestly offering might be marred. Yet one point of comparison is valid. Christian ministry is, for all sorts of reasons, a risky business. Those called to it need our prayers for their protection, and our support if it brings them to grief.

5 'Unclean, unclean!'

Leviticus 13:9–46

Serving in the temple was not the only duty of Israel's priests. They had also to instruct God's people (e.g. Leviticus 10:11). In today's passage, and in others nearby, it seems, at first sight, that they were also public health officers and quarantine officials!

However, this is to misunderstand their role here. Scholars are pretty clear that whatever the condition they were to investigate was, it could not have been leprosy, or 'Hansen's disease'. The symptoms mentioned in these chapters don't match those of that horrible, transmittable affliction. Nor can Hansen's disease be passed on to textiles (Leviticus 13:47–59) or houses (14:33–54).

Could it have been psoriasis whose symptoms resemble the condition described in Leviticus? If so, why should this noncontagious disorder require isolation? Well, if holiness and purity are linked to life, then, by the same token, impurity is bound up with death. In its severe form – where the body is discoloured and the skin flakes – psoriasis resembles the changes that occur after death. As such, in a community pursuing holiness, sufferers would be an anomaly, neither truly dead nor fully alive. So, plausibly, it was out of concern for the purity, the holiness, of God's people, rather than public health, that the priests examined and isolated sufferers.

Nothing here suggests that the 'leper' had necessarily done anything wrong. Furthermore, it is strongly implied that the condition will prove temporary; that God will act to heal and cleanse (Leviticus 14). Yet the fate of the innocent sufferer, banished into an albeit temporary 'social death' (13:46), remains pitiable. We should recall that those enduring this cruel fate seem to have been a special priority in the healing ministry of Jesus.

Through no fault of their own, they found themselves banished 'outside the camp' so that the 'holiness' of God's people could be maintained. What might they have thought about their situation? Many, no doubt, were understandably bitter and aggrieved. But might some have come to a place where they accepted their own fate, so that others could continue to enjoy fellowship with God?

We may recall that, as Hebrews 13:12 reminds us, Jesus also 'suffered outside the city gate' to sanctify God's people. Was it simply compassion that led Jesus to single out lepers? Or was it also fellow-feeling?

6 The holiest of days

Now we reach the chapter which is placed right at the centre of Leviticus, and thus, because Leviticus is the middle book of the five 'Books of Moses', the centre of the entire Pentateuch. Given the importance of the rituals of this 'Day of Atonement', the placing is almost certainly deliberate.

Many of us will be familiar with the outline of what happens on this most high and holy day – the sanctification of Aaron (and after his death, the High Priests that followed him) by bathing and by sacrifice; the selection of two goats, one to die as a 'sin offering', the other to be released into the desert, carrying 'all the people's sins'. This complex set of rituals allows the High Priest to enter into the very presence of YHWH in the 'holy of holies', there to 'make atonement', not just for his own iniquities and uncleanness, but also for 'the people'. Meanwhile, the entire people are commanded to 'deny themselves' (traditionally understood as to follow a strict fast).

Much of this is familiar; above all, the belief in the purifying and sanctifying power of blood. However, some things remain puzzling; the role of the released goat is particularly enigmatic. It is sent 'to Azazel' (in verses 8, 10 and 26 – the rendering 'as a scapegoat' is misleading). Who, or what, is Azazel? It's not clear. Possibly this is some sort of demon; in which case the sins laid on the goat's head belong to him, but cannot be used against the people in this uninhabited place.

Be that as it may, the complexity of the rituals and the severity of the fast are markers of how seriously Leviticus takes the failure of God's people to obey his command and the need, accordingly, for confession and atonement. It is astonishing to reflect that at the centre of the Pentateuch is not a celebration of how God's people have successfully followed God's instructions for holiness, but rather an elaborate recognition of their failure. Furthermore, given that it must be repeated annually (verse 29), even this complex rite offered only temporary and partial cleansing.

However, 'he [Jesus] has appeared once for all at the end of the to remove sin by the sacrifice of himself' (Hebrews 9:26).

Guidelines

'Poor, little, talkative Christianity', so Mrs Moore, in E.M. Forster's novel *A Passage to India*, unfavourably compares 'western' faith to the profundity she senses in a great cave, a Hindu holy place. It's easy to dismiss Forster's carefully crafted comparison as a cheap jibe, but this is one of those criticisms we do well to pay some attention to. It's a bitter paradox: the more we have striven to make our churches cheerful, accessible, welcoming and inclusive, the more they have been deserted. But then, why should anyone want to come to places which are simply chatty, superficial and unhallowed? Which lack any sense of what Rudolph Otto called 'the numinous' – the overwhelming sense of that presence, not ourselves, which makes for righteousness?

Western Protestants are often drawn to other Christian traditions that seem more profound than their own. However, the tremendous mystery of the divine cannot be conjured up by rituals, by 'bells and smells', though, yes, it can inhabit them. As it can inhabit a charismatic congregation caught up in the Spirit in its worship songs; or a bare, unadorned Calvinist chapel steeped in prayer.

Leviticus does not suggest for a moment that the mechanical performance of its rituals can ensure that we are brought safely into God's awesome presence. The book assumes throughout that YHWH is mysterious and powerful beyond our imaginings, as well as loving and good, and that only those who approach him with a sincere heart can endure his holiness. In our journey through the book, we have come to its holy centre. We shall see that the holiness it seeks to promote in worshippers must follow through in transformed lives marked by purity and loving intentions.

- When did our worship last make us aware that the Holy One of Israel was among us to save and bless?
- When did we last sense the nearness of Christ, divinely powerful yet infinitely loving, in our prayers?
- What role do confession, attentive waiting and silence play in our spirituality?
- How can scripture help us when we feel we are simply 'going through the motions'?

1 Where do we meet God?

Leviticus 17:1–8

The restriction of sacrificial offerings to one place – the 'tent of meeting' in the wilderness wanderings; later, the Jerusalem temple – is another unique feature of Israelite religion. We should note that this restriction only refers to sacrifices; in mind here (verse 5) are the peace offerings, that is, those shared in feasts. Indeed, Deuteronomy 12:20–21 specifically permits the 'non-sacrificial' slaughter of clean animals for food when Israelites are living in places remote from Jerusalem.

However, permitting only one legitimate altar would have seemed very strange to most people in an ancient world where there were temples in many places, to many gods. Moreover, reading the biblical histories, it seems clear that, before Jerusalem was established as the place YHWH 'chooses for his name to be honoured', faithful Israelites could also sacrifice to YHWH at the local 'high place' near any settlement of God's people (e.g. Judges 6:25–27; 1 Samuel 16:1–5).

How come? Well, verse seven offers a plausible rationale that follows on from Israel's restriction of worship to the one true God, YHWH. The temptation to try and serve the false gods as well as YHWH remained an ever-present danger throughout Israel's history. So, this command seeks to ensure that idols could not be served under cover of the permission granted in Deuteronomy 12. No, if you were near the legitimate altar, there you must go, so the priests could ensure that your offering was directed to the true God. Fascinatingly, in view of the 'scapegoat' ritual in the previous chapter, the false gods in view here are described simply as 'goats' (Hebrew se'arim), usually rendered 'goat-demons' in the English versions.

Scripture everywhere insists that God cannot be limited by time and space. Paradoxically perhaps, this truth was not contradicted, but reinforced, by allowing only one legitimate altar. Solomon's words when he inaugurates the temple – 'heaven and the highest heaven cannot contain you, much less this house that I have built!' (1 Kings 8:27) – reveal a deep awareness that we cannot restrict God within our buildings, no matter how desperately our idolatrous hearts seek to do so. 'For thou within no walls confined/inhabitest the humble mind' (William Cowper).

2 Respecting the boundaries

Leviticus 18

Sexual desire, in itself, is never condemned in Leviticus, or anywhere else in scripture. Indeed, the Song of Songs celebrates the passionate, physical love between a man and a woman. However, like all good things, human sexuality can be abused, and precisely because it is such a powerful force within us, that abuse can come to dominate and degrade not only individuals, but societies. They can become 'sexualised'; that is, sex can enter areas where it should never be allowed to intrude.

The introduction to this chapter (verses 1–5) is, accordingly, of great importance for understanding it. YHWH commands Israel to be a different sort of society than the one they left, ancient Egypt, and the one they are going to, Canaan. In both these cultures sexuality had broken its bounds and intruded into areas that it should not have gone into.

Among the elite in ancient Egypt incestuous relationships were not regarded as abnormal. Recent DNA investigations have demonstrated that the famous pharaoh Tutankhamun (1341–1323 BC) was the product of a union between his predecessor Akhenaten and Akhenaten's sister. A later ruler, Ptolemy II, boasted that such transgressive relationships were proof of the semi-divine nature of Egyptian royalty, who were not bound by the ordinary rules of humanity.

If, in Egypt, sexuality was allowed to intrude inappropriately into the world of the family and the court, in Canaan it made its way into the heart of religion. The sexual union of the god Ba'al and his consort Asherah was held by the Canaanites to lead to the fertility of the land. Such understandings of the divine role were widespread throughout the ancient Near East, and led to the practice of 'sacred prostitution' in which transgressive sexual activity in 'holy' places mimicked, and thus encouraged, the gods. That such transgression also encouraged the breaking of other taboos, including that which bids parents cherish their children's lives above all things (v. 21), should not come as a surprise.

Those who dismiss the strict boundaries Leviticus 18 seeks to establish in these matters as the morality of the Bronze Age would do well to ponder the ever-increasing sexualisation of our own societies; that most abuse of children occurs within a domestic context; and that, sadly, sexual scandals are not unknown within the household of faith.

3 No holiness but social holiness

Leviticus 19:1–18

The Day of Atonement may be central to Leviticus, and, indeed, to any understanding of biblical holiness; but it is not the peak from which the only way is down. Rather, as we go through the book, the notion of holiness both intensifies and expands.

The intensification is partly through repetition in which we are led back to things that have already been encountered. Our passage today begins with words that recall important elements in the ten commandments of Exodus 20 and then harks back to the peace offerings of Leviticus' early chapters. Significantly, both the commandments selected (which refer to family life and corporate worship) and the sacrifices (whose meat is shared with others) focus on interpersonal relationships. They serve, then, as an introduction to the verses that follow; ones that draw out the implications of living together in the presence of a holy God (v. 1).

Holiness cannot stay confined within the temple. It must flow out into our life together. It must produce a society in which the vulnerable are cared for and protected (vv. 9–10, 13–14); one in which truth-telling and justice are standard (vv. 11–12, 15–16); in which disputes are settled amicably and rationally, and the vendetta is outlawed (vv. 17–18). The final words of verse 18 are, of course, singled out by Jesus as the second of the key biblical commands, one that is 'like unto' the first, to love God (Matthew 22:39, KJV).

Many claim today that they 'do not need to go to church to be a good person' and point to the hypocrisies of churchgoers to prove their point. Such accusations are too often valid ones. But what if our very ideas of what is good are based, even if we do not recognise it, upon glimpses of the goodness and holiness of the God revealed in scripture? Some societies, ancient and modern, regard compassion and care for the vulnerable as mere sentimental weakness, and glory in the cult of the strong and successful; in passionate love of self, untouched by concern for others. If we think that the values of this passage are self-evident, we should consider those of ancient Rome, or North Korea.

How aligned is what we say and do on Sunday morning with what we do and say on Monday?

4 Sanctifying time

Leviticus 23

The passages omitted cover a rather bewildering miscellany of topics. Some (rules for priests and offerings; sexual morality) deal with topics already mentioned; others, for instance, the prohibitions of mixing different kinds of cattle, seeds and cloth (19:19) are puzzling (perhaps these were pagan practices, symbolic of a perverse readiness to transgress boundaries). These wide-ranging statutes insist that holiness must cover the whole of life. Agriculture, food, trade, tailoring; all are areas in which God's people are to remember his holiness and live differently, righteously, because of him.

If everything must be oriented towards God, so must time itself. The seventh day of every week is to be hallowed by rest and gathering together (23:3), as a regular reminder of God's care for his people and his presence around their homes. We are, perhaps, so accustomed to the rhythm that this seven-day cycle imparts to our own lives that we find it difficult to imagine living without it. Yet many other ancient cultures had 'weeks' of ten or eight days, and even those (e.g. in Babylon) that had seven-day weeks had no regular day of rest.

Festivals were indeed celebrated in all ancient cultures, each one generally dedicated to one particular god. Once again, however, Israel's calendar was unique in that all of its festivals were directed towards one God, YHWH. We should note how the number seven (and its multiples) marks out the dates of the festivals (23:5, 15, 24, 27, 34, 39, 41–42) and that the seventh month of the year is especially holy. This number is, of course, particularly linked to God's activity, not least in creation (Genesis 1). Furthermore, Passover (23:4–8) and the Feast of Booths (23:43) reminded Israel of YHWH's gracious deliverance of their ancestors from bondage in Egypt.

In our culture 'holy days' have become 'holidays'. True, Sundays, by and large, remain quieter, but that just makes it easier to shop; Christmas and Easter are promoted as times for conspicuous consumption. I suspect that these changes have played no small part in encouraging the disorder, the lack of helpful structure, that has harmed many modern lives.

What can we do to make it clear that all our time is devoted to God?

5 The great reset

Leviticus 25:1–34

The number seven, as we have already seen, has a divine significance. Never more so than in this chapter, where it is used to bring the whole land promised to God's people to a state of holy rest (25:1–7). Underlying everything commanded here is the belief that this land does not belong to them, but to God (25:23). The people only hold it on, as it were, leasehold terms; God is the freeholder. The sabbatical seventh year reminds them that they cannot do what they want with this precious resource loaned to them. It has to be allowed to rest, to lie fallow. This will indeed ensure its long-term health, but even more important is the lesson that it is not theirs to do with as they see fit; that, ultimately, their thriving in the land depends not on their own efforts but on their trusting obedience in the One who has brought them into it (25:18–22).

The same lesson is reinforced by the year of Jubilee when all land was 'redeemed', that is returned to the original clan (extended family group) to which it was allocated when Israel entered the land (some of the details of how this was to work are found in Joshua). Interestingly, many scholars assert that a periodic cancellation of all transactions involving land could never have actually happened. Leviticus, they argue, merely portrays an unrealistic, unworkable ideal. This, perhaps, reveals more about academics, and our difficulties in imagining different economic arrangements from those in affluent modern cultures, than it does about the practicality of Jubilee. We need only assume that any 'purchase' of land would have been a time-limited lease to see that it would have been difficult but doable.

This understanding that 'the earth is the Lord's' (Psalm 24:1) has much to say to us today. Were we truly to realise that we hold the earth in trust, and that our own stay upon it is time-limited, how our arrogant abuse of its resources, as if they were ours forever, might end!

What do we need 'to let lie fallow' in our societies, and, indeed in our own lives? What needs to be redeemed?

6 Promises, promises…

Leviticus 27

At first sight it may be surprising that Leviticus ends with what might seem, once again, to be trivia: with regulations, most of which involve what should happen when people dedicate themselves, their animals or their property to YHWH. Yet, in fact, these passages align well with the book's central concern for holiness. Being holy, in the understanding of Leviticus, is nothing less than keeping our promises, as God keeps his.

Such promises are never to be taken lightly. This is clear from the cost of trying to 'row back' on those made, perhaps in haste and under pressure ('Oh God, if you let me live, then I will serve you forever…'). If an Israelite were, indeed, to dedicate their whole life to God formally, perhaps using the words of Psalm 116:16–19, and were then to wish to go back on this solemn vow, then they would have to pay considerable sums for their release from such obligations (27:1–8 – a shekel is a weight in silver approximately corresponding to a month's wages). If animals or objects are to be 'redeemed', then a fifth is added on top of their value (27:13; see the mechanism for determining the value of land in the light of the Jubilee in 27:18–25). A similar penalty is added if tithes of goods and animals are redeemed. We will recall from the dreadful story of Jephthah and his daughter (Judges 11:29–40) how costly rash vowing can be; although Jephthah's failure to avail himself of the mechanisms outlined here for redeeming dedicated people seems incomprehensible.

Nevertheless, Leviticus does not forbid vows. When a man publicly promises to be faithful to a woman, or vice versa; when a politician vows to serve faithfully in the office to which they have been elected; when someone solemnly states that they will 'tell the truth, the whole truth and nothing but the truth'; then these vows should be fulfilled. When they are not, serious damage is done to the commitments that hold us together and allow us to thrive. However, this chapter calls us to consider very carefully the obligations we take upon ourselves.

Have we 'over-committed' ourselves? What promises should we not keep, if necessary, compensating others appropriately for our failure? What vows should never, under any circumstances, be broken?

Guidelines

How have the readings we've shared over the last fortnight affected you? At the risk of making some unjustified assumptions, did you hesitate a little when you saw that our subject was to be Leviticus? I hope that you now feel more interested in, and intrigued by, this book; that its insistence on several important biblical themes has repaid your investment in time and attention. Such themes include the importance of offering things to God with a glad and obedient heart; God's holiness, and the demand he makes upon us to try to imitate it (Leviticus 19:2), although that attempt will so often end in failure; in the willingness to be countercultural when our culture denies God in what it honours and celebrates. These themes remind us that God's love and mercy must never be understood in a sentimental and complacent way. His grace, though it abounds, is no cheap and easy thing. It is mediated through costly, sacrificial means.

Over the last weeks, the fellowship group that meets in our house has been (at their own request, let it be said) reading through Leviticus. Although we wanted to do this, several members of the group admitted that they approached the book with some trepidation. It's true that, as we have seen in our own journey through the book, there are some passages that might trigger painful reactions. However, the overwhelming experience of the group has been positive. In particular we discovered, again and again, passages that shed life on the New Testament's witness to the ministry and person of Jesus. The purity of his holy life reveals to us what it means to imitate God in a rich and full way; the willing obedience with which he went to his death completes and fulfils all that the temple sacrifices point to.

- Have we received new insights into God's holiness and Jesus' righteousness through our reading of Leviticus?
- Has reading these passages from Leviticus encouraged us that other scriptures we find difficult might have something to say to us?

FURTHER READING

Mary Douglas, *Leviticus as Literature* (Oxford University Press, 1999).

John Goldingay, *Exodus and Leviticus for Everyone* (Westminster John Knox Press, 2010).

Gordon Wenham, *The Book of Leviticus (New International Commentary on the Old Testament)* (Eerdmans, 1979).

Mary Magdalene: mad, bad and dangerous to know?

Siobhán Jolley

Mary Magdalene is one of the most widely known figures in Christian tradition. Yet, despite her enduring appeal, we find surprisingly little information in the New Testament to flesh out the character who has captured the attention of scholars, believers and creatives for centuries.

The sexual sinner and prayerful penitent that many people call to mind when they think of Mary Magdalene is the product of myth and reception rather than a character easily identified in the pages of scripture. Indeed, a very significant portion of our understanding about Mary Magdalene is based on content that comes from beyond the biblical text. Pope Gregory the Great's Homily 33 is often held responsible for perpetuating two major misconceptions: first, that Mary Magdalene, Mary of Bethany and the unnamed woman who anointed Jesus in Luke 7 are the same person, and second, that Mary Magdalene was a sexual sinner. The woman in Luke 7 is simply described as 'a sinner', with no explicit sexual connotation, but Gregory's interpretation established a precedent for linking her to sexual sin that has proven nearly impossible to forget.

So, what does the actual content of the gospels reveal about Mary Magdalene? Over the course of this week of reflections, we will explore what the biblical texts tell us about the woman who Luke introduces as a key part of the community ministering with Jesus, and who, according to Matthew, Mark and John, remains present throughout his death, burial and resurrection. We will consider stories that have been used to form part of the wider popular myth and reflect closely on the texts which tell us about whom the biblical Magdalene was. Far from 'mad, bad, and dangerous to know', we will meet a faithful friend, wise witness and apostle to the apostles.

Unless otherwise stated, Bible quotations are taken from the NRSV.

1 Dissociating the sexual sinner

Luke 7:36–50

The Magdalene's feast (celebrated on 22 July) was added to the western Christian calendar by Bede in c. 720 and by the time Masses were offered in her honour in the tenth century, the sexualised sinner reading was widely established. This text was the prescribed reading until after the liturgical reforms of the Second Vatican Council in the 20th century. It is no surprise, therefore, that his passage is one that so many readers call to mind when asked to think about Mary Magdalene, and is a key part of the line of thought which associates her with being a sex worker.

Though this story appears just before Luke introduces Mary Magdalene, there is no suggestion that we should identify her as this woman. That conflation can be traced to Gregory the Great's Homily 33, where he states that this woman, Mary Magdalene and Mary of Bethany should be understood as one and the same. Yet, even if we do accept the idea that this woman should be understood as Mary Magdalene, there remains no textual evidence that she is a sexual sinner. Though there are some sexual connotations to the anointing woman's loose hair and physical contact, both of which cross social boundaries of expectation with a male stranger, the nature of her sin is never stated. The term *hamartalos* does not refer to sexual sin in particular, and the fact that she is 'known in the city' still demands an exegetical leap to decide that this is a euphemism for (professional) promiscuity.

In fact, this text is the story of a woman whose reputation precedes her, but who demonstrates enormous courage to act in faith despite this. She expresses contrition through weeping, and repentance through bathing Jesus' feet in her tears and anointing him with oil. As soon as he sees her interacting with Jesus, Simon thinks he knows what type of woman she is, but his description fails to do her justice. In this, and the parallel versions of Matthew and Mark, she is defended from criticism by Jesus and praised for her actions. This is the story of a flawed woman who shows more faith than the men who criticise her. How ironic, then, that her story has been misapplied to the tale of Mary Magdalene, who has been similarly maligned.

2 Seven demons?

Luke 8:1–3; Mark 16:9

Mary Magdalene is introduced in Luke 8:2 and Mark 16:9 by the detail that she is one 'from whom seven demons had gone out'. However, we do not get any explanation of what this possession entailed. In his 591 Homily 33, when he conflated Mary Magdalene, Mary of Bethany and the woman from Luke 7:36–50, Gregory the Great argued that the seven demons represented 'all the vices'. Given the symbolism of seven as a sign of completeness, it makes some sense to assume that the seven demons are supposed to indicate something all-consuming – i.e. that she was totally sinful or totally ill. Yet, there is equally no reason for us to expect the gospel writers to be euphemistic here.

Demon-possession was an almost universal belief in the Mediterranean world of the New Testament. Spirits are a frequent affliction of Lukan women in particular (including Peter's mother-in-law in Luke 4:38–39 and the stooped woman healed by Jesus in Luke 13:11) and in Luke 8:2, Mary is named at the head of a whole list of women cured of evil spirits and infirmities. The idea of healing in this context can be understood as restoring an ability to function socially, rather than the particularities of medical health as understood today. Despite our colloquial use of the term 'demons', the scholar Gerd Theissen warns against reading spirits in the New Testament as referring to mental illness. He argues they should be understood as something affecting the entire person (which may incorporate mental illness, but cannot be exclusively understood as such).

Whatever Mary Magdalene's demons were, and whatever the social implications, the gospel accounts do not dwell on the events of the past. Rather, the label is used as a distinctive feature to identify her among other women (and even other Marys). It clarifies that *she* is the follower of Jesus who accompanied him from Galilee to the tomb, witnessed the resurrection and was subsequently sent out as an apostle to the other apostles. Regardless of her past, the gospels depict Mary Magdalene as someone who is fully ready, willing and able to serve as a devoted disciple of Jesus in the present moment.

3 Mary called Magdalene

Luke 8:1–3

These three short verses are among the most important for establishing Mary Magdalene as a follower of Jesus. They affirm that she, along with other Jewish women such as Joanna and Susanna, accompanied Jesus during his ministry and supported him out of their private means. Jesus and his followers were itinerant, leaving work and family behind, and lived from a common purse (John 13:29). It seems clear that these women were, to all intents and purposes, funding Jesus's ministry. More than this, Luke tells us that they 'ministered' too.

We know from Luke's account that there were more than twelve disciples (see, for example, the sending out of the 72 in Luke 10:1–23) and the ministry and support provided by these women surely places them into this category. The term *mathetes* appears around 260 times in the gospels and Acts, to describe those who are present 'with Jesus' (Mark 3:14; Luke 9:18; Luke 22:56), who hear Jesus' teaching (Mark 4:33–34; 10:23–45) and who perform ministry such as healings and exorcisms (Mark 6:7–13). The nature of their role has been a source of great scholarly dispute, but it is almost universally agreed that Mary Magdalene and the other women were essential to the practical and material success of Jesus' ministry.

Another argument for Mary as a disciple is found in her name itself. It is unlikely that Mary was even from the place that we know as Magdala, and Joan Taylor has argued convincingly that 'Magdalene' is a form of nickname meaning 'tower-ess'. Such names were relatively commonplace among the disciples, used to mark significance when referring to attributes of their character or to indicate those who have left their hometown. Perhaps the most obvious example is that of Simon being called Peter. Simon was one of the most common names of the age (like Mary) and so it makes sense that he would be given a distinguishing appellation given his importance in the church. As 'Peter' indicates Simon's steadfastness, so 'Magdalene' might indicate Mary's uprightness. If we follow this line of reading, then Mary Magdalene is very much the opposite of mad, bad and dangerous to know! Rather, she is a close disciple of Jesus, who is praised for her upright character and example to others.

4 At the foot of the cross

John 19:17–30

Across the Passion accounts, there is an emphasis on female witness. Luke flags the presence of the women among the onlooking acquaintances (Luke 23:49); Matthew and Mark go further still, identifying the group of women witnesses as a distinct group (Matthew 27:55–56; Mark 15:40–42). Here, John's account identifies Mary Magdalene as among those at the foot of the cross by name in verse 25. She is not looking on from a distance but stands with his closest disciple and his mother as Jesus is crucified. But what is it that she is witnessing here?

The violence functions almost implicitly in the narrative because the story is so familiar, but the scene that Mary Magdalene is placed within is one of torture and state execution. Even when we think about the details of such a violent death, the familiarity of the account and our knowledge of Jesus' resurrection protects the reader from the magnitude of the situation. However, Mary Magdalene is watching this brutality for the first time as it is exercised towards someone who she has followed and served, and with whom she has developed a profound relationship as faithful friend and devoted disciple. Dori Laub, a psychiatrist and trauma survivor, has explained that bearing witness to such violence has a material and traumatic impact, where the witness experiences physical echoes of the confusion, dread and injury that the victim might feel. This exists in addition, therefore, to the personal trauma that Mary Magdalene is experiencing individually as she begins to process her own shock and grief. There is an additional traumatic burden of empathy – she is in a very real sense suffering alongside Jesus.

Despite the horror that unfolds, Mary Magdalene remains. Unlike in the other gospel accounts, there is no physical distance – she is as close as it is possible to be to the violence and brutality of Jesus' sacrificial death. More than this, she watches not just his death, but also his burial. Just as John 13:1 notes that, 'having loved his own who were in the world, he loved them to the end', so Mary Magdalene remains a faithful witness to the end – and beyond.

5 A weeping witness

John 20:1–16

In this passage, Mary Magdalene is still experiencing trauma. She has witnessed brutal violence enacted against her beloved friend, yet still returned to the scene of that harm to do her duty in anointing his body. Her grief and trauma are compounded by its absence. Trauma is materially compounded in the body, and the physical effects behave as if the trauma is current. Even returning to the tomb would necessarily recall the previous visit, witnessing his burial, which would readily induce the memory of the preceding violence. Furthermore, according to John 20:27, Jesus' body still bore the marks of his violent death, so it would hardly be surprising for the sight of him to trigger a trauma response.

This trauma response is evidenced by Mary Magdalene's distress and weeping (which is mentioned twice, in verses 13 and 15). Early interpreters such as Celsus read this as evidence that she was a hysterical or emotionally volatile character. However, Shelly Rambo has interpreted this detail of Mary Magdalene crying as a recognition that her witness is 'forged through' her tears. The same Magdalene who has experienced the compounded trauma of being at the foot of the cross is the first witness to the resurrection and thereby the first bearer of the core message of Christianity.

We see the same pattern repeating itself across John's account: approach, message, disbelief. She approaches the tomb and bears the message to the disciples, and they doubt her; then Jesus approaches her and (as we will see when we read on) she bears his message to the disciples, and they doubt her once more. Yet, despite this, she perseveres where the men do not; they flee, and she waits once more. This waiting, despite her pain, trauma and even doubt, is rewarded by a relationship with Christ. He calls her by her name – a beautiful moment in this story where she has mistaken him for a gardener or a stranger. She knows his call, and he knows her, and with that, her courage is renewed once more. Though the pain endures, so does love, and it is this that results in the weeping witness being the first observer to Jesus' miraculous triumph over death.

6 Apostle to the apostles

John 20:17–18

Across the gospels, Mary Magdalene is consistently presented as the first witness to the resurrection. However, this is also consistently her final appearance in the gospels and, indeed, the New Testament as a whole. Jesus gives Mary specific instructions to bear witness, but we do not learn about the male disciples' response. Perhaps we can infer all we need to from the fact that John goes on to describe how the resurrected Jesus seeks out the men who are hiding and doubting, and that Mary Magdalene disappears entirely from the narrative once her emissary role is complete.

Scholarship has fallen broadly into two camps when appraising the exact meaning of Jesus' command that Mary Magdalene should not hold on to him. Some argue for a purely metaphorical reading of Jesus' words – that it is about clinging emotionally to a past or a temporary reality, rather than physically touching him. On the other hand, physical interpretations are more inclined to recognise intimacy. Rudolf Bultmann, for example, sees her reaching towards Jesus 'as a friend would do to a friend who has come back again'. Could both be correct? The grieving Magdalene might seek a metaphorical connection to the past, spiritual intimacy with Jesus *and* physical contact. There are any number of reasons why these are plausible, human responses to this extraordinary situation.

Whatever happens in their encounter, Jesus still trusts Mary Magdalene to take the news of his resurrection to the apostles. Moreover, we know that women still had an important role to play in the early church. Paul's letters provide clues about the roles played by women in the community and in churches, and Elisabeth Schüssler Fiorenza has suggested that Mary Magdalene ought to be understood similarly. She argues that the writings of the New Testament conceal a leadership rivalry between Peter and Mary Magdalene, a conflict that saw Peter ultimately prevail. The absence of Mary Magdalene at the end of John and across the remainder of the New Testament reminds us how speculative such an argument is. Nevertheless, the fact that Mary Magdalene is specifically sought out and sent out by Jesus in these verses gives us grounds to uphold her, at the very least, as apostle to the apostles.

Guidelines

In the New Testament, Mary Magdalene is mentioned on twelve separate occasions, at the head of a list of women associated with Jesus or as apostolic witness to the resurrection. The only contextual information found in the synoptic gospels regarding the Magdalene, apart from her name and her discipleship, is the reference to 'seven demons' cast out of her, which is found in Luke 8:2 and repeated in the longer ending to Mark in 16:9. Though not identified as Mary Magdalene, it is commonly understood that the Mary of John 11:1–44 and 12:1–11 is the same character. Less convincing is the link to the sinful woman in Luke 7:36–50, which arises as a result of Gregory the Great's Homily 33.

Ultimately, we know very little about the historical Mary Magdalene and, over 2,000 years apart from the life of Jesus, we are unlikely to uncover definitive answers. With close and careful readings of the texts, however, we are equipped to ask better questions, challenge received narratives and think anew about the significance Mary Magdalene held in the Jesus movement and the earliest Christian communities.

When we set aside the myth, misremembering and muddle of Marys, what we do know from the New Testament is not insignificant. She was a disciple of Jesus; a significant part of a group of women who supported Jesus' ministry (and may have even had a ministry of their own); a faithful friend through Jesus' life, suffering and death; a selfless witness to the crucifixion; the first witness to the resurrection; and apostle to the apostles. Far from someone mad, bad or dangerous to know, these texts paint a vital picture of a relatable role model for believers today.

FURTHER READING

Philip Almond, *Mary Magdalene: A cultural history* (Cambridge University Press, 2022).

Diane Apostolos-Cappadona, *Mary Magdalene: A visual history* (Bloomsbury T&T Clark, 2022).

Susan Haskins, *Mary Magdalen: Myth and metaphor* (HarperCollins, 1993).

Christian giving

David Spriggs

During the next two weeks we will explore some texts which relate to the way we as Christians should be giving our money for God's work. Threaded throughout scripture we find stories, laws and guidance about this.

I believe that our giving really matters in the context of *Guidelines*. Guidelines states, 'Its intention is to enable all its readers to interpret and apply the biblical text with confidence in today's world, while helping to equip leaders as they meet the challenges of mission and disciple-building.'

Christian giving hits both these targets. An essential aspect of every Christian's discipleship is that we should not only give but learn to give in truly Christian (we could add 'Christ-like') ways. In our complex domestic and often pressurised financial worlds, it is easy to allow materialism and acquisitions to dominate our lifestyles, whether this is through the ease we can purchase anything online 24 hours a day or the bombardment with appeals to support good causes that saturate our screens, whether on TV or phones, adverts or major programmes. Pausing from these pressures by engaging prayerfully with scripture is a necessary discipline to enhance our Christian giving.

But Christian giving is also significant because of its mission impact. Just as we humans can't function without food, water and air to breath, so our Christian missions – whether those of the local church, community charities, national organisations or international organisations – cannot function without the necessary funds.

I offer these biblical reflections with the prayer that they might challenge us all as believers and enable those who preach, to encourage congregations to enter into the joy of giving.

Unless otherwise stated, Bible quotations are taken from the NRSV.

1 Giving and discipleship

Mark 1:16–20; Luke 19:1–9

Martin Luther observed, 'People go through three conversions: the conversion of their head, their heart and their pocketbook. Unfortunately, not all at the same time.' Our two readings show that sometimes these can be closely related and, when they are, it has powerful effects.

The first passage relates the encounter of Jesus with Simon Peter, Andrew, James and John, which led to them becoming disciples. They were all fishermen. It wasn't guaranteed that they would haul in a catch and so be able to adequately feed their families. Other gospel stories show us that sometimes they could fish all night and catch nothing, and that on other occasions they would be thwarted by violent storms. Fishing was a good but an unstable source of income. They were far better off, however, than the many 'day labourers' who turned up in the marketplace at dawn and hoped they would be employed – if not, they had no income that day. James and John seem to have had a more extensive business, as they had hired workers as well as being in partnership with their father.

The call of Jesus meant Andrew and Simon Peter gave up their nets and James and John their boat. Two ways of saying that they surrendered their capacity to earn! What a risk they were taking for themselves and their families.

Zacchaeus' encounter with Jesus shows that his 'conversion' entailed a complete rethink of his attitude to finances. As a chief tax collector in Jericho, he was financially in a very comfortable position. Jericho was a major tax collecting city and Zacchaeus was benefitting from a team who were working for him and all paying him for the privilege. To fund this, they were having to extort additional money, over and above that which the Romans demanded and the extra they already added on for their personal benefit. His encounter with Jesus freed Zacchaeus from the wealth and security, not to mention the sense of power, which his career gave him. This is in sharp contrast to another Lucan character we meet a few verses earlier, 'a certain ruler' who was, 'very rich', and refused to surrender his wealth (Luke 18:18–25).

These stories and associated sayings from Jesus encourage us to ensure that people's conversion includes the surrender of their possessions, their income and their future prospects.

2 Giving and Christian mission

Acts 2:42–47; 4:32–37; 11:27–30

Yesterday's stories indicate that Christian discipleship brings freedom from bondage to financial resources and pressures. They also indicate ways in which a proper attitude to wealth impacts Christian mission. The disciples could only become involved with Jesus' mission because they were no longer employed. And Zacchaeus' words and actions showed the power of Jesus to change behaviour as well as releasing many others from the oppression they experienced.

Today's passages confirm Jesus' power to transform our attitudes to wealth and show how this contributes to the mission of Christ.

Acts 2:42–47 indicates the real sense of community into which converts entered. Some, perhaps many, were those who had come from the Diaspora to Jerusalem for the feasts of Pentecost and, before that, Passover; they would have stayed with relatives. Once they converted to Jesus, some of them may have experienced hostility. They found sustenance and security in the Christian family. But to make this possible, others had to sell their property. Later we hear about Barnabas, who sold a field, but he is part of a much bigger movement (4:32–37).

Acts tells us not only about the financial basis for this remarkable, deep and extended sense of community in the early church in Jerusalem but also about the emotional basis for this. They 'ate their food with glad and generous hearts, praising God and having the goodwill of all the people' (2:46–47). Acts suggests that this model of inclusive and supportive community was itself a powerful factor in the growth of the church. Sadly, we know this model was not without its problems. Acts 6:1–2 indicates the problems of felt injustice, while Acts 5:1–11, the Ananias and Sapphira incident, tells us that not everyone reached the same level of financial freedom.

Such supportive communities have been part of the church's story through the ages, and still today provide a challenge to develop missional communities of care and inclusivity.

Our final passage reminds us that while this form of community may not have continued in Jerusalem beyond the first few years or been a hallmark of Christianity in the Gentile world, nevertheless, this spirit of abandoned generosity was part of the church's DNA. The Antioch church sent financial help to Jerusalem. This kind of 'collection' will feature more later!

3 Tithing – love not law

Tithing – the giving of a tenth – is a well-known Old Testament command, embedded in British culture with the historic 'tithe barns' and a marker of valid discipleship in some Christian churches. For some, it can also be seen as indicative of commitment to the whole Bible as 'the Word of God'. One of the best-loved texts for those who are 'pro-tithing' is Malachi 3:8–13. Those who don't tithe are 'robbing God'; honouring him financially will result in prosperity for the giver and admiration by 'all the nations'.

This is a complex topic but here are a few things to bear in mind.

The Deuteronomic account of tithes is fascinating because it indicates that for two out of three years the beneficiary of the tithe is the giver. It was to provide them with a feast at the temple; only in the third year was it 'given away' to provide for the Levites. Maybe, however, we should remember that those of us who give to our churches also benefit from doing so!

Tithing was by no means all that an Israelite gave to God – there were many sacrifices and feasts where they contributed, but again the giver was often a beneficiary of the gift – not only receiving forgiveness but also in terms of feasting. It is also not clearly defined what the donor was meant to tithe. Grain and fruit probably – but what about fish caught in the sea or money earnt by carpentry? So, in our modern society should we tithe all our income or deduct our housing costs?

Jesus was scathing about those who were meticulous in their tithing (even small amounts of herbs) but neglected matters of 'justice and mercy and faith', although he adds that they shouldn't neglect tithing. His image of them straining out gnats and swallowing camels embeds itself in our memories, as does his pen-picture of the Pharisee whose boastful stance before God includes, 'I give a tenth of all my income' (Luke 18:12).

There is little to suggest that disciples in the early church were expected or required to tithe. The Council of Jerusalem in Acts 15 does not stipulate that tithing was required from Gentile converts (vv. 19–21, 28–29). While the focus of the discussion was about circumcision, the decision indicates that wider issues were also considered.

4 Attitude and amount

Luke 20:41—21:4

Attitudes and perspectives in God's kingdom are very different to those of the surrounding culture. This comes out time and time again in the ministry of Jesus. In many ways, the kingdom of God is, from our human perspective, a 'topsy turvy' world. This applies to our attitudes to money and wealth in the kingdom of God and beyond that to our actual Christian giving.

Mostly, people look to their assets to give them a sense of security. Owning your own home is much more secure than renting one. Having significant savings or stocks and shares is much less worrying than only having bills and debts to deal with. But Jesus encourages us to not store treasure on earth but in heaven (Matthew 6:19–21). Those who can afford to drive around in flashy cars (or collect them in their extensive garage!) or buy designer clothes usually want to be seen in them as it adds to their sense of 'esteem'. The same can be true of generous donors both in the communities around us and within the church. Jesus was well aware of these attitudes and comments on them with great incisiveness both here (Luke 20:45–47) and elsewhere (Matthew 6:1–4). His encounter with the rich young ruler (Luke 19:16–26) and the ensuing conversations with the disciples underline the dangerous 'entrapment' of our wealth. The foundation for Christian giving, then, is that we imbibe a kingdom perspective on wealth, otherwise we shall not be free to make the right decisions either for our planned and regular giving or for more spontaneous or occasional opportunities.

Kingdom perspectives affect not only attitudes but our assessment of amounts! If we are looking for large amounts to fund a church mission project or to sustain a charity, it is natural to be delighted to receive big donations, but in the story of the rich givers and the poor widow we see Jesus' evaluation. From the kingdom perspective, her two copper coins are more than the thousands of pounds from a wealthy donor! Jesus evaluates not by amounts, perhaps by percentages of total wealth and assets, but rather by the heart attitude from which the giving flows. Not only did the two copper coins cost the widow more, but they indicated a deeper trust and love for God than the wealthy. The rich givers were probably seeking praise (Luke 20:46), whereas she was giving out of love.

5 Sacrifice not surplus?

Deuteronomy 8:7–20

In this passage, Israel is challenged to always keep in mind the long journey that God had brought them on. They are especially to focus on the fact that ultimately God has given them everything: 'Do not say to yourself, "My power and the might of my own hand have gotten me this wealth." But remember the Lord your God, for it is he who gives you power to get wealth' (vv. 17–18).

He has led them through the wilderness and provided for their needs; he is bringing them into a fruitful land; he is making their animals and crops fruitful; he has given them the abilities and energy to farm successfully. The conclusion is that all they achieve, possess, enjoy and own are not their achievement but God's gift.

This perspective on life leads to the conclusion that everything we have belongs to God and he has the right to it all.

It is all too easy in our current culture to emphasise our achievements and the fact that we have the right to all we earn and so to dispose of it as we choose. We can resent paying taxes (whether income tax, NI, Council Tax, VAT, etc.) because we forget that without security we could not function, without rubbish collections we would be over-run by vermin, without healthcare we couldn't work anyway, without trade relations we couldn't import and export. Equally, given this culture, we slip into the attitude that as everything is our achievement, we are being magnanimous to give to Christian work out of our surplus – once we have spent all we want to do on ourselves – it's ours anyway!

One of the dangers of giving along the lines of 'tithing' is that it can re-enforce this. I've given my 'commitment' to God, so the rest of my income and possessions are mine! I suggest that a more biblical approach to Christian giving is to recognise that everything is from God and, as his servants, we should use it all in ways that honour him, whether spending, saving or giving.

For Christians the grounds for this perspective are not only that God has given us all our abilities and the benefits of the nation and community in which we live, but also that he has rescued and renewed us through Christ, who gave his all to make this possible.

6 The collection for God's people

1 Corinthians 16:1–4

The most comprehensive insight into Christian giving in the New Testament is found in 2 Corinthians 8—9; we will focus on this next week. But these verses towards the end of 1 Corinthians provide a helpful bridge into these chapters. They give us a glimpse into the life of the churches. The key is verse 2: 'On the first day of every week, each of you is to put aside and save whatever extra you earn, so that collections need not be taken when I come.'

The background to this collection (although here it is to avoid collections!) is that Paul was committed to raising money to provide for the Christians in Jerusalem probably during a time of famine (Acts 11:27–30) or because, as Christians, not only were they persecuted (Acts 8:1b–3) but they were also pushed away from their Jewish family and communities, which would have made it harder for them to work and trade.

The Greek word for 'collection' was thought to be used only in biblical Greek but has since been discovered in the papyri where it usually relates to taxation, i e. legally required giving. However, careful study has shown that Paul often emphasises the voluntary and not compulsory nature of this collection. As well as its compassionate and practical benefits, it is probable that Paul saw this collection missiologically – as some Old Testament scriptures referred to the wealth of the nations flowing into Jerusalem.

We need to note that we cannot directly equate giving to our church or denomination with the teaching about the collection, but we can nevertheless discern several guiding principles for Christian giving in general.

The reference to 'the first day of the week' is interesting in that it brings to mind the Christian communities worshipping on Sunday (compare Revelation 1:10), although here it is not explicitly about them taking their gift to their worship but rather the discipline of setting money from the previous week's earnings. As temples were used for slaves to save their money towards their release, it may be that Paul envisaged individual monies being kept safe in the place of worship. The motive for this regular weekly discipline is to avoid the necessity for a collection when Paul arrived. It indicates that our giving should be regular and organised rather than depend on urgent or emotionally driven appeals.

Guidelines

- Acts gives several indications of the community in the early church that provided for everyone's needs and was funded by people selling their possessions, including land and donating the proceeds to the church. It also mentions some problems that arose. Consider examples from the history of the church as it has attempted to 'replicate' this kind of deep community – the monastic movements, the Moravians, to-day some missional communities in urban situations etc. Do you think local churches can offer models of this 'generosity'?

- Are there less demanding approaches which carry some of these principles that you know of? Housing projects for homeless people (e.g. Hope in Action) and free meals at 'Warm Spaces' are two which come to mind.

- Are these a) helpful in modelling freedom from financial bondage, b) stimulating us to work out contemporary embodiments as local churches c) focusing our prayers?

- Do you see any evidence that these approaches impact the mission of the church?

- One of the Old Testament models for giving by God's people was the 'tithe'. To what extent do you consider this to be a sound biblical model for churches now?

- Review Jesus' comments and hints relating to tithing. How can we encourage responsible, proportionate Christian giving without falling into the traps Jesus noted?

- What allowances do you think we should make (for ourselves or others) if we wish to apply this principle today? Should we, for instance, take away from the income we tithe things like mortgage payments (should we then 'tithe' the value of our estate in our will?), childcare, travel to work?

- How do we factor tax payments into our 'tithable' income? Does 'gift aiding' provide a mechanism for this?

- How can we encourage people to feel the freedom to give significant amounts (compare Barnabas) and at the same time honour and welcome the 'costly' but small gifts (like the widow) in our churches?

1 The grace of giving

2 Corinthians 8:1–4

In this passage Paul holds up the 'churches of Macedonia' (likely including Philippi and Thessalonica) as an example and therefore stimulus, to emulate or indeed challenge the Corinthians to surpass! We know from Paul's letter to the Philippians that he affirms them for their generosity both in the service of the gospel and towards him personally (Philippians 4:15–20).

This Corinthian passage clarifies the purpose of this collection: it is a 'ministry to the saints' (v. 4). It is clear that the collection is not for the upkeep of the temple in Jerusalem, or for Paul's own evangelistic mission, and this description makes it likely that he has the money for the Christian communities in Jerusalem in mind. In 2 Corinthians 11:7–10 Paul emphasises that he had never asked the Corinthians to support his evangelistic ministry financially ('I proclaimed God's good news to you free of charge') but that the Macedonian churches had done this. This indicates a second objective for Christian giving – to resource the mission of God.

Paul refers to the generosity of the Macedonians as the outflow of 'the grace of God that has been granted' to them (v. 1). The background to this understanding is that the Macedonians gave 'during a severe ordeal of affliction' (v. 2). Whether this connotes persecution or famine is not clear, but it means that their generosity is not measured by the amount they gave alone (although it seems this was significant) but by the relative cost to them – a principle we have already noted (see v. 3). Another principle is that they gave 'voluntarily' (v. 3). This is emphasised by verse 4, 'begging us earnestly for the privilege'. It was not under compulsion or moral blackmail that they gave – they wanted desperately to be allowed to give. It was not reluctantly but earnestly wanting to be involved; it wasn't a duty or burden, it was a privilege.

No wonder, then, that Paul sees in this approach to giving 'the grace of God that has been granted to them' (v. 1). This attitude to giving is not simply human nature, it is a spiritual gift (see Romans 12:6–8, especially verse 8).

Giving, whether to strengthen the life of the church, to facilitate the mission of God or to relieve poverty, to provide education and healthcare or to enable more independence among poorer communities, is primarily a spiritual opportunity not a financial task.

2 Giving ourselves first

2 Corinthians 8:5–9

This passage contains the pivotal verse not only for Paul's understanding but for all Christian giving. The NRSV loses the theological connection in verse 9 when it translates 'grace' as 'generous act' (although see footnote; note also this usage in verses 6 and 7). Here is the NIV: 'For you know the grace of our Lord Jesus Christ, that though he was rich, yet for your sake he became poor, so that you through his poverty might become rich.'

Whereas Paul began chapter 8 by saying, 'We want you to know… about the grace of God that has been granted to the churches of Macedonia,' now he says, 'For you know the [grace] of our Lord Jesus Christ'. Because Paul recognises that Christian giving is fundamentally a divine activity, he grounds his appeal in the reality of the gospel. It is the appropriate outworking of being a disciple of Jesus Christ that we give; it is modelled on his 'generous act'. There is certainly a place for motivating people to give by recounting stories of other people's generosity (the Macedonians), but the primary motive is the reality of the gospel.

This 'knowing' then is not merely historical knowledge; it is deeply personal knowledge. It is embedded in us as Christians by the reality of the good news we heard and the salvation we have received.

What is equally noteworthy is that Paul uses more human motivations to stimulate the Corinthians to give. Throughout his correspondence with them he has been tackling, in many ways, their tendency to regard themselves as superior to other Christians within their community (e.g. who baptised them – 1 Corinthians 3:1–9, spiritual gifts – 1 Corinthians 12—14) and to other churches beyond (and to him). They consider that they 'excel in everything' (v. 7). Here he challenges them to prove their superiority by excelling in the grace of giving. He makes this clear, 'I am, by mentioning the eagerness of others, testing the genuineness of your love' (v. 8). What we do well to note, however, is a clause in verse 7, 'and in our love for you'. More naturally it would have been 'your love for us'. But Paul wants to avoid any possibility that he is trying to get them to give to benefit himself or his team. Christian giving should not be motivated by any benefit we ourselves might gain, including the kudos of major projects accomplished.

3 According to our means

Paul has a problem! It seems that the Corinthians had previously promised a substantial contribution for the collection he was making from the Gentile churches to relieve the needs of the mother church in Jerusalem. The Corinthians had probably promised to give the most – they always wanted to excel. It also seems likely that they had made a good start, then their enthusiasm waned and they stopped building their collection altogether. We don't know why this problem occurred. Maybe it was simply that they 'ran out of steam' – like the hare that dashed off and then the excitement went out of the process, it was a longer haul than they expected. Maybe they got off quickly because they expected Paul soon to pick up their offering. As Paul didn't turn up, they wondered whether he ever would. Maybe the relationship between Paul and the Corinthian Christians turned sour. After all, he does have a lot of hard, even harsh, things to say to them.

His solution is not to 'command' them, because giving should be a matter of freedom, not obligation. He does, however, want the money they have promised, not for himself but for the Jewish Christians. Hence, he gives 'advice'.

He therefore goes back to remind that they used to have a desire to give (v. 10). He seeks to reconnect them with their initial motivations they had caught the vision, but it had become dull. Christian giving will require people to be reminded of the heart feelings they had when they started, especially if it is a long haul – to buy an expensive piece of equipment, such as a bus that can be used as a base for youth work on estates, a building project to provide a welcoming and attractive café environment as a meeting place for the community or to build a school in an African village.

He comes up with two overlapping principles that can stimulate our Christian giving. First that we should give according to our means, i.e. in the light of what we have, not what we don't have. Christian giving is not dreaming. If we are unrealistic about what is practically possible, we may lose our way. Second, it is about appreciating the discrepancy between what we have and what the beneficiaries don't have. We need to be realistic about our relative wealth in the light of their real need (vv. 13–14).

4 Completing our commitments

2 Corinthians 8:16—9:5

'A promise means nothing, until it's delivered' – I thought that was a brilliant strapline for a parcel delivery company, and I think Paul would agree with the sentiment. In this passage, he deals with the challenge of completing the collection in two ways.

The first is ensuring that he and all involved deliver on their promise to get the money safely to the famine-stricken Christians in Jerusalem so they can benefit from the generosity of those Gentiles who have given for this purpose (8:16–23). In order to establish the reliability of the messengers, he underlines their credentials. Titus has the same level of intense commitment to the Corinthians as Paul himself has. His going to Corinth is not only because Paul has instructed him, but he is eager to go voluntarily. Another unnamed 'messenger' has different credentials – he is a proven and effective evangelist, but has also the imprimatur of the churches. The way Paul puts this suggests that he is independent of Paul. Whereas Titus was one of Paul's 'buddies', this second person isn't but has been authorised by the churches. A third person's dependability has been tested by Paul, but if there is a distinguishing mark for him, it is that he has vouched for the Corinthians – which might imply he is 'on their side'.

What Paul is seeking to ensure is that the Corinthians can give with the confidence that there will be many checks and balances among the team who will physically carry their collection on the long and hazardous journey. People who give should expect that their money will reach its target audience without undue deductions in the process and that it will be used as stated. If we expect people to give to our church or to a project overseas, we should be as careful in ensuring they can have confidence in the process.

The second is getting the Corinthians to deliver on their promises – for without that, the collection will be significantly diminished (8:24—9:5). Again, there are a number of ways he does this. First, he emphasises that how adequately they give will be known among the churches more broadly. Second, he affirms and reminds them of their good intentions (eagerness). Third, he leaves them with no excuse – they are being alerted, with adequate warning that the time to fulfil their commitments is fast approaching. Providing clear notice is helpful for financial 'success'.

5 Sow generously, reap generously

2 Corinthians 9:6–9

This passage contains one of Paul's clearest indications about the nature of Christian giving, in verse 7: 'Each of you must give as you have made up your mind, not reluctantly or under compulsion, for God loves a cheerful giver.'

First a comment about the apparent contradiction. If we *must* give, doesn't that imply there is some kind of compulsion; whereas Paul goes on to say we are not to give under compulsion? This refers to external pressures. The obligation implied in this 'must' indicates it is imperative that the giver does this out of his own free will, once he has worked out what under God he should do. The 'must' relates not to the amount given but rather to the necessity of following the principle of doing it freely.

We therefore need to pay careful attention to what is meant by 'as you have made up your mind'. The Greek idiom refers to the heart. But it is clear from the associated verb 'has decided' that here, as often in the Bible, 'heart' refers not to our feelings but to our volitional decisions. Hence our giving should not be driven by the emotive impact of the way the appeal is presented (as is often the case visually on television ads by secular charities), but careful and deliberate considerations of our resources, our requirements, the example of God in Jesus Christ and the relational obligations we may have to those who will benefit from our giving – in this case the bond of Christian fellowship between the Christians in Corinth and the mother church in Jerusalem.

We are not to give 'reluctantly' either. More literally this is 'out of pain'. That is, we are not to give to avoid the pain (perhaps of guilt) or even a sense of inadequacy if we don't. Maybe the intention is that we shouldn't give more than we consider appropriate simply because others are giving more.

What is of great significance is that Paul grounds his statement not on psychological factors but on God's own nature. As scripture indicates, God loves a 'cheerful' giver. In Job, this word is used of the man who has been rescued and restored by God (Job 33:26). So, the cheerful giver is the person who is enjoying the liberation of doing what he knows God wants. Such a person need not be anxious because God will more than compensate for his generosity (vv. 8–9).

6 Giving produces thanksgiving

2 Corinthians 9:10–15

This passage, and therefore our understanding of Christian giving, now takes a rather surprising turn! All along Paul has been encouraging the Christians to resume and fulfil their intention to give generously to add to the collection he is taking to relieve the needs of the Jerusalem church. He assures them that they won't lose out by being exceptionally generous, because God will more than compensate them (v. 10). This is not a promise of financial prosperity (give to God/our ministry and you will become wealthier and healthier!), but a 'harvest of righteousness'.

However, his main motivation is projected into the future. He wants them to sense the difference that their giving will make. If you give then research will lead to medical care for patients – you will save lives. Your giving will enable a person with reduced sight to have a guide dog and enable them to regain a lot of independence. Your giving 'supplies the needs of the saints' (v. 12). But his main pull is quite different. 'You… will produce thanksgiving to God through us', this ministry of giving 'overflows with many thanksgivings to God' (vv. 11–12)

It is neither the Corinthians nor Paul and his team who will receive the thanksgiving but God. Giving for Paul is ultimately not a financial but a spiritual and theological issue. That does not diminish the compassionate and practical nature of giving and its impacts, but it heightens its significance. Our human giving has a divine dimension. Paul has frequently used the word 'grace' to refer to the act of giving financial aid, usually rendered, 'generous act/undertaking' in the NRSV. There is a linguistic connection in Greek between this and the word for 'thanksgiving' which is missing in English. This reinforces the theological point. As so often with Paul, his arguments lead to an outpouring of praise (see for example Romans 11:33–35; 15:9–12)

This climaxes in a rich and memorable reference to Jesus, 'Thanks be to God for his indescribable gift!' (v. 15). If these two chapters were a symphony, this would be the celebrated climactic end. Here Paul reveals the deep place of his heart. Everything is in response to the incredible generosity of God expressed in the ministry and mission of Jesus, which he had personally experienced on the road to Damascus and which the Gentiles know because they have been enfolded in the plan and mercy of God.

Guidelines

Paul's correspondence with the Corinthian church about the 'collection' provides us with some wonderful scripture verses and suggests principles we can consider both for our own Christian giving and the way we help our churches and Christian communities to give.

- Pray through some of the verses that have caught your attention.
- Here are some of the key insights I noted:
  1 The grace of giving
  2 Give themselves first to the Lord
  3 Acceptable according to what one has
  4 Complete your commitments
  5 Sow generously, reap generously
  6 Give what you decide
  7 Give freely and cheerfully

- How helpful do you find these thoughts? Which two are the most challenging? Can you encourage others to grow through them? Would you add anymore?
- Bearing in mind the teaching of Jesus, are there any that you think might be misunderstood, misapplied or have potential pitfalls?
- These chapters also present some interpretative problems. How relevant are they to a local church congregation when these chapters are all about charitable giving which is limited to Christians (to help the poor in Jerusalem)? Is it appropriate to transfer them to local congregations to support the local church or denomination?
- What difference do you think more considered Christian giving could have on the growth of your local church and the global mission of the church? Are their steps you could take to promote this?

FURTHER READING

Ralph P. Martin, *2 Corinthians (Word Biblical Commentary 40)* (Word Books, 1991).

Keith F. Nickle, *The Collection* (SCM, 1966).

Andrew Roberts, Neil Johnson and Tom Milton, *Gladness and Generosity* (BRF Ministries, 2018).

R. V. G. Tasker, *2 Corinthians* (IVP, 1969).

Dealing with difficulty

M. J. Kramer

Most of us like to hide our problems. We prefer to foreground our strengths and keep our weaknesses and challenges discreetly under wraps as we present ourselves to the world. Yet one of the most compelling aspects of our faith is that for Christianity this is not the case. For Christianity places its greatest problem perpetually at the centre of our attention.

The hardest of all challenges to faith, the problem of suffering, the question of how to believe in God in the face of so much human pain, finds its most profound symbolic expression in the crucifixion. For here, the one person of whom it could truly be said 'he has done no wrong' experiences the most profound torture.

Far from hiding away from this problem, the church places this symbol of our greatest paradox constantly before our eyes on our altars, our church buildings, our prayer books, our necklaces and in our art.

For Christians, therefore, to ignore suffering or to seek to solve it with easy answers must be anathema to our faith. Rather, the contemplation of suffering is one of the central aspects of how we seek to live out a vocation to be God's faithful people.

These reflections are a contribution to this lifelong calling. Drawing on a series of rich biblical narratives, they ask how the sufferings we observe in the Bible can help shape how we understand the relationship between suffering and God, others and ourselves.

Bible quotations are taken from the NRSV.

1 Where is God?

Genesis 21:1–21

The first tears mentioned in the scriptures are those of Hagar. This seems appropriate, as in this poignant story we hear of the emotional and personal cost not only of human jealousy but also of God's plan of election of the children of Isaac.

In her feminist reading of the text, Mayer Gruber makes the intriguing suggestion that we should understand God's command to Abraham as being to 'listen to' Sarah's feelings, rather than to 'obey' her instructions (v. 12). The Hebrew, she claims, could mean either. As Gruber points out, this solution has the advantage of acquitting God of responsibility for casting Hagar out into the desert. Yet, such a solution seems a little too convenient and comfortable.

For people of faith there is always the temptation to suggest to those in difficulty that God can only be the solution to, not the origin of, our plight. Like Job's 'comforters', we can sometimes lapse into suggesting that God is only responsible for the good, happy, encouraging, just and positive things in our world, leaving those suffering angry that the creator of all seems to be able to evade responsibility for a darkness that they not only perceive but also experience.

Stories like those of Hagar demand a more sophisticated response. Here we see God as involved in both Hagar's predicament and in her consolation. God's plan of election, when lived out in the human world, results in challenge and pain as well as hope and possibility. Here God appears not simply as a projection of our wish-fulfilment but as one, transcendent and mysterious, who takes responsibility for the difficulties as well as the joys of our world.

Yet if God is a source of Hagar's trial, he is also the one who provides her with the relief that makes it endurable, and the two ways in which he does this are significant for our own engagement with suffering. First, God encourages Hagar to look to the future, to recover hope, to recognise that present sufferings are not how it will always be: 'I will make a great nation of him' (v. 18). Second, God opens Hagar's eyes to see that water which her distress had prevented her from noticing (v. 19). Even in the most difficult time, there is, somewhere, a well from which to drink.

2 Difficult memories

Numbers 11:4–20

One of the most profound ways in which the Bible can help us in times of struggle is by providing us with stories of difficulty in which we can recognise ourselves and the many ways in which stress and anxiety can affect our behaviour and our thinking.

In this passage from Numbers the Israelites are physically and emotionally exhausted, and in their fragile state they start to remember their previous life in Egypt. The lengthy list of items of Egyptian food in verse 5, introduced by repeated Hebrew formula (*ve-et-ha*, 'and the… and the… and the…') powerfully evokes the Israelites' appetite for their past in Egypt. Yet the most telling word in this verse is one of the shortest: *hinnam* ('for free'). In the light of their present suffering the Israelites have developed a rose-tinted memory of the past. The suffering and slavery of Egypt has, seemingly, been forgotten, and the land of oppression is remembered instead as a place of free food.

God's reframing of the Israelites' complaint in verses 18–20 exposes the reality of this distorted thinking. Their complaint implies that things were better for them in the land of Egypt and that they are wondering 'why did we ever leave?' The experience of the Israelites helps us to notice how in difficult times our own memories of our past, and our perception of alternative lives we might have led, can so easily become distorted: 'everything was so perfect back then,' or 'it would have been so perfect if only…' God's response reminds us to be realistic about our past, and to be wary of the idealised 'memories' and imaginings that can lead us to believe that our present is the worst of all possible worlds.

The striking maternal imagery which Moses uses about himself (v. 12) highlights one of the difficulties and dangers of trying to support those in need. The temptation to provide everything, solve everything and fix everything for others in distress can quickly become overwhelming, even if we seek to do it with the best of intentions. Indeed, it can even be counterproductive for the people we care for, as they regress to the state of infants carried in the bosom. God's solution, to empower others to assist, keeps us from both the anxious exhaustion and the narcissism of sole responsibility.

3 Companionship in suffering

Few biblical characters are as closely identified with their sufferings as Naomi. Indeed, in verse 20, Naomi herself claims that her name, the very thing that gives her identity, should be changed from Naomi ('pleasant') to Mara ('bitter').

Yet if Ruth 1 dramatises one of the most complete biblical examples of suffering, it also presents one of the most radical examples of care for one in distress. At the heart of the chapter, we find two different responses to Naomi's grief-stricken determination to return home. Orpah bids her mother-in-law farewell. This decision is not criticised by the narrator. Rather, Orpah's farewell kiss is a sign of an affectionate and respectful parting (1 Kings 19:20). Orpah has simply reached the limit of the care she can offer. Ruth, however, takes a different path.

Naomi's demand that Ruth and Orpah return home is couched in a series of rhetorical questions. As Frederic Bush notes, these do not represent a logical assessment of possible options for the future. Rather, they are an expression of impossibility and despair. Ruth seems to recognise this. She makes no attempt to reason Naomi out of her situation, to encourage her to look on the bright side, or to try to problem-solve. She simply offers her committed companionship.

The verb used for Ruth's response in verse 14, to cling, is used for the deepest kinds of commitment, such as marriage (Genesis 2:24). The depth of this commitment is then reinforced by Ruth's poetic assertion of allegiance to Naomi, as the same Hebrew words are repeated first to refer to 'you/your' and then 'me/my' (vv. 16b–17a). Here Ruth does not promise Naomi any outcome, or any particular future. She simply promises to be with her, whatever the outcome may be.

The freeing nature of this kind of care can be seen in the arrival at Bethlehem. Commentators often note that Naomi ignores Ruth's presence at this point. I would emphasise equally the fact that Ruth is content to remain silent. She allows Naomi to speak of her feelings without interruption, knowing that in this situation the most important thing is not to be noticed, but simply to be there.

Even if we are unable to make Ruth's radical commitment to those in distress, her example shows the importance of persistent presence, listening and commitment, over seeking to solve others' problems or argue them into happiness.

4 Difficult truths

Luke 3:1–20

Despite the fact that Luke summarises John's words as being full of encourage-ment and good news (v. 18), John the Baptist's cry must have been difficult to hear. Yet, this is a different kind of difficulty from those explored so far. For it is a difficulty that is spiritually necessary.

Matthew directs John's harsh opening words, 'you brood of vipers', to the Pharisees and Sadducees who join those seeking his baptism (Matthew 3:7). In Luke, this rebuke is applied to the 'crowds'. John's is a discomforting message that needs to be heard by all. Spiritual apathy, in Luke, is not the preserve of a religious elite, but a challenge we all need to be shaken out of.

Luke, uniquely, gives a series of examples of what it might mean to 'bear fruits worthy of repentance' (v. 8) which demonstrate the moral dangers of being too comfortable with how things are in our world. John's demand to those of us who are wealthy to share our belongings (v. 11) reminds us of the too-easily-ignorable fact of the number of people who go without what we regard as basic necessity.

These dangers become even more acute in his next two examples. Tax collectors are told to only collect the amount prescribed, and soldiers are told not to threaten, to extort money or to make false accusations. The implication is that it is easy for corruption and injustice to become casual and routine. 'But everybody's up to it, aren't they – I don't want to miss out!'

Sometimes we need to be shocked out of our complacency, and harsh words, embarrassment and pain can sometimes have that effect. Yet the preacher prepared to speak these difficult truths can bring great difficulty on themselves as well. The reading ends with a foreshadowing of John's own martyrdom. His integrity costs him his life.

John's words remind us that it is not always the function of faith to make us feel better about ourselves. Rather, sometimes being a person of faith makes our life more difficult. In the end, Luke's summary is correct. John's harsh words of justice remind us that the good news is only really good news if it is good news for everyone.

5 Praying in distress

Luke 22:39–53

Christians are often told that the correct response to times of suffering is prayer, which will bring assistance and relief. Yet the idea that true prayer will reliably provide comfort is challenged in Luke's account of Jesus' prayer on the night of his betrayal.

In Luke, simple relief from 'pain' (*lupe*, a more generic term than the word 'grief' in contemporary English) comes not through prayer but through sleep (v. 45). At first this seems strange. We tend to think that pain causes insomnia. Perhaps Luke is making a more general point that oblivion of some kind is one response to pain. For us, when in pain, seeking oblivion might take other forms: we might turn to distractions, to overwork, to risky behaviour, or to alcohol, or to withdrawal, avoidance, and denial. All of these might seem to be a refuge from our sufferings.

Prayer, however, is not this kind of escape. The prayer of Jesus in this reading is described literally as 'agony' (*agonia*, v. 44). The word, which occurs only here in the New Testament, is used for the struggle and effort of competition and battle as well as mental distress. The intensity of this prayer is further evoked by the physical description that as Jesus prayed his sweat fell like drops of blood.

The authenticity of verses 43–44 has long been questioned, as they are absent from about half of the manuscripts of Luke. Nevertheless, even if they are not original, they are a sensitive expansion of verse 41. For Luke only describes someone as kneeling for prayer if it is a prayer of great effort and intensity (e.g. Acts 7:60).

This passage, therefore, challenges the idea that prayer brings instant relief from suffering. That is the province of sleepy oblivion. Prayer here, rather, is a particularly acute form of perception in the presence of God. Prayer is facing up to reality in the company of the One who really IS.

This is not easy, but it is valuable. The un-praying disciples in verses 49–51 respond to danger with impulsive and random violence. Without waiting for Jesus' response to their question, one of them lashes out ineffectually at an innocent slave. If we do not face the reality of our suffering in prayer, we too might be tempted to take out our pain unthinkingly on others.

6 Beginning again

Acts 9:1–19a

Paul's conversion on the road to Damascus is one of the most familiar of biblical stories, and the fact that Luke tells it three times in Acts demonstrates its importance. Recent commentators, moving away from earlier psychological approaches to the experience, have highlighted the theological themes of the passage. Nevertheless, while this moment marks the beginning of Paul's new vocation, it is also a moment of profound physical and emotional dislocation for the saint.

Usually in a divine encounter of this kind, the prostrate human character is offered some kind of immediate reassurance such as 'stand up' (Ezekiel 2:1) or 'do not be afraid' (Revelation 1.17). Here, however, Paul is left perplexed at first: 'Who are you, Lord?' (v. 5). Moreover, Paul falls to the ground, is struck blind for three days and starves himself (the word is not the usual one for a religious fast, perhaps emphasising the emotional aspect of this withdrawal from food) and loses his strength (v. 19). Worst of all for someone like Paul, the sense of agency and purpose with which he was busily occupied at the opening of the chapter has been completely destroyed. Now he must be led by the hand (v. 8) and receive care from others (v. 17–18).

I do not believe the emotional turmoil of this story is incidental to the change that takes place within Paul. As Richard Rohr points out in his book *Falling Upward*, it is sometimes only suffering that is beyond our control that has the power to shake us out of our accustomed habits, to contemplate life afresh and to begin once again. Paul's reduction to helplessness in this story, his descent to the depths of difficulty, enables him to interpret his past afresh and rebuild his life on new foundations.

Read in this way, Paul's experience is familiar to many of us for whom a difficult time has brought about a new beginning. While the pain of these times is never a good thing, and never something we should seek, with hindsight we come to recognise that times of difficulty can also be the birthplaces of new possibilities, new ways of living and new hope.

Guidelines

- How do you think of God in times of difficulty? Do you only see him as responsible for the positives, or do you see him as implicated in the difficulties you are facing? Is lament and anger ever part of your relationship with him?

- When you are struggling, how do you think about the past or alternative choices you might have made? Are you realistic about the challenges as well as the advantages of all possibilities? Or do you fall into thinking 'the grass is always greener on the other side'?

- How do you care for others who are suffering? Are you able to offer them attention and companionship? How easy do you find it to avoid jumping in too quickly with solutions to their problems, or with attempts to make them see the positive side of things?

- How do you respond to criticism? Most of us are initially defensive when we are challenged. How do you try to enable yourself to be attentive to voices that identify ways in which you could change, grow, or develop?

- How do you experience prayer? Can you pray in difficult times or do you try to find distractions to avoid facing into the difficulty? Do you feel you can be honest with God?

- Have you had an experience which has made you start again in life? Have difficult times ever led to new possibilities for you, or for those you love? How would you feel if you, like Ananias, were called to assist someone in a difficult but potentially life-changing time?

FURTHER READING

Mayer I. Gruber, 'Genesis 21.12: A New Reading of an Ambiguous Text,' in Athalya Brenner (ed.) *A Feminist Companion to Genesis* (second series) (Bloomsbury 1993), pp. 172–181.

John Goldingay, *Genesis* (Baker Academic, 2020).

Adriane Leveen, *Memory and Tradition in the Book of Numbers* (Cambridge University Press, 2008).

Phyllis Trible, 'Human Comedy,' in *God and the Rhetoric of Sexuality* (Fortress Press, 1978).

Frederic W. Bush, *Ruth, Esther* (Word Biblical Commentary) (Zondervan, 1996).

David Lyle Jeffrey, *Luke* (Brazos, 2019).

Craig S. Keener, *Acts: An Exegetical Commentary* (4 volumes) (Baker Academic, 2012–2015).

Richard Rohr, *Falling Upward: A spirituality for the two halves of life* (Jossey-Bass, 2011).

Luke 17—24: the way of peace

Loveday Alexander

These notes are being written more than a year before you read them, at a time when the news is full of 'wars and rumours of wars' (Matthew 24:6, NRSV) – in Ukraine, in Africa, in the Middle East. It's hard to believe there will ever be a peaceful resolution. Over the next three weeks, we will be reading the final chapters of Luke's gospel, written in a world full of the rumours of war. Most scholars believe that Luke was written in the wake of the disastrous Jewish Revolt of AD66–70, when the Jerusalem temple was destroyed by the Roman army and its sacred vessels carried in triumph to Rome, along with thousands of Jewish captives who were sold into slavery. Luke's readers would have known about this: if you lived in Rome (as many of them did), it was impossible not to know what had happened. Many in the community would be traumatised; many would be thirsting for revenge, wondering if God had let them down, longing for God to assert his kingly power.

Yet Luke's gospel begins with a vision of peace: of God's mercy, of the 'dawn from on high' breaking in, of the one who comes 'to guide our feet into the way of peace' (Luke 1:78–79). Luke's gospel is written in the belief that in the person of Jesus, God has 'raised up a mighty saviour for us' (literally: a 'horn of salvation'), to fulfil the prophecies that 'we would be saved from our enemies and from the hands of all who hate us' (Luke 1:69–71). In this final section of the gospel, we begin to see the cost of the path of peace that Jesus must tread.

Unless otherwise stated, Bible quotations are taken from the NRSV.

1 Stumbling-blocks

Luke 17:1–19

Our reading of Luke's gospel picks up at the end of Jesus' teaching ministry in Galilee. Ever since 9:51, Luke has been reminding us that Jesus is 'on the way to Jerusalem' (v. 11). So, in these final chapters, there is both a sense of danger as the journey gathers pace and of urgency. Jesus is moving towards his appointed end; time is running out to grasp the true nature of the kingdom he preaches.

So, there's a note of warning in these final nuggets of teaching for the disciples (v. 1), sober advice for a time when they will have to work out for themselves what it means to follow Jesus without his physical presence. 'Occasions for sin' (v. 1, 'scandals' in Greek) are bound to come, even among Jesus' followers. The church will have to find a way to take seriously the possibility of abuse and the damage it causes to the innocent 'little ones' (v. 2), while remaining open to the possibility of repentance (vv. 3–4).

There's a note of realism too: disciples are in it for the long haul (vv. 7–10). When my daughter was small, I remember coming in from the shops with a loaded pram and a hungry baby, just longing for someone to sit me down and make me a nice cup of tea. But Mum was 200 miles away – I just had to get on with the job. Following Jesus is a grown-up pursuit – sometimes serving the master means just seeing what has to be done and getting on with it without looking for applause.

But there's a note of hope as well. Faith can work wonders – even the tiniest grain (vv. 5–6). And even the most unpromising ministry can open up the way for God to act (vv. 11–19). Between Galilee and Samaria (v. 11) lies the valley of Jezreel (Esdraleon), one of the great battlegrounds of the biblical world. Through it ran the 'way of the Sea', the great highway linking 'Galilee of the Gentiles' to the coastal plain. It's an 'in-between' place, a place where the marginalised drift into the spaces where nobody wants them. Jesus' act of healing reaches out to those on the margins, without discriminating between Jew and Samaritan. But it's only the 'foreigner' (v. 18) who has the faith to see the salvation that Jesus is offering (v. 19).

2 Thy kingdom come

Luke 17:20–37

Where is the kingdom of God? This wasn't a theoretical question for Jesus and his contemporaries. It was an urgent, here-and-now question about real life. You can feel it pulsing through this chapter. When is God going to *do* something? When is God going to sort out the mess we're in – make people respect his laws – bring in that wonderful reign of peace and justice that we read about in the prophets? When is God going to start putting the world to rights? How long, O Lord, how long? We've all asked those questions at one time or another… and it's the right place to start. We have to begin by recognising that this world – for all its wonder and beauty – isn't how God meant it to be.

But what does Jesus mean by saying 'The kingdom of God is among you' (v. 21)? Within you? Within your grasp? Asking 'Where is God's kingdom?' can be an easy way of blaming the world's problems on someone else. Whether the problem on our hearts is climate change or world peace, putting the world to rights has to start with realism and repentance, identifying what's wrong and acknowledging our own contribution, both to the problem and to the solution. The kingdom of God begins with you and me. We can only pray 'Thy kingdom come' if we're prepared to let God be king in our lives, our relationships and our communities.

But we can also make the opposite mistake of thinking that everything depends on us – with the danger of remaking the world in our image, using force if need be. It's easy to get taken in by fake messiahs claiming to be putting the world to rights. There's an old cartoon by Calman, showing God leaning down from heaven and shouting, 'Love one another – or I'll come down and thump you!' That's often what we have in mind (unconsciously) when we pray for God's kingdom to come. But God's way of putting the world to rights involves something much more costly. God's kingdom – God's promised king – was there, walking among them. Jesus' challenge (then and now) is to recognise the Son of Man in our midst and the costly way of peace he came to bring.

3 Like a child

Three stories about prayer. Who gets closest to God? Who does God listen to? Not who you might expect!

Pray with persistence seems to be the message of the first story. Bishop James Jones used to say that this parable was a favourite with the families of the football fans killed in the Hillsborough disaster, who had to fight so hard to get justice for their loved ones. They cheered when they heard the story of the old widow who *never gave up* – and eventually got justice by sheer determination. Not that God is 'like' the unjust judge – parables don't work that way. This is a 'how much more' story: even the most corrupt and case-hardened official will listen in the end, if only to shut you up. How much more your heavenly Father who loves you? Keep praying: your instincts are right. There *is* a God, and he *does* care about justice. God's kingdom will come in the end.

Pray with penitence is the message of the next story: *just come as you are.* The story of the Pharisee and the tax collector doesn't fit our easy stereotypes of bad guys and good guys. But Jesus' teaching is more subversive. Not that good and bad don't matter – on the contrary, God cares passionately about truth and justice. But the starting point for coming close to God is knowing how much we need him – like a child, like a baby, we reach out for God's love because we need it to survive. A 'goodness' that's all wrapped up in itself will just get in the way. Real goodness is self-forgetful, aware of its desperate need for God's mercy. C.S. Lewis used to say, 'I pray because the need flows out of me all the time, waking and sleeping. It doesn't change God, it changes me.'

Pray with simplicity is what it comes down to: *come as a little child.* A young woman once said to me, 'Oh, I know it's too late for me – you have to come to Jesus as a little child or not at all.' But that's not what Jesus meant! It's not about *when* you come to God – you can come at any time, from childhood to old age. It's about *how* you come. There's something about the directness and simplicity of children that Jesus saw as a parable of how we all need to come to God – open, direct, trusting, just as I am.

4 Through the eye of a needle

Luke 18:18–43

Is it a coincidence that the Bank of England in London is based in Thread-needle Street? Jesus' joke about the camel trying to get through the eye of a needle has become part of our language. I like the African version of this story, about the monkey who sticks his skinny arm into an empty kerosene tin to grab a fistful of nuts – only to find he can't get his fist out of the narrow hole. Treasure can easily become a trap.

Jesus has a lot to say about the dangers of 'storing up treasures for yourself' (compare Luke 12:13–21, or the parables of chapter 16). But throughout much of the Bible, riches are seen as a sign of God's blessing (compare Psalm 112). What's wrong with being rich? Jesus highlights two problems, interlocking but distinct. There's the problem of ill-gotten gains: getting rich by extortion or fraud (like Zacchaeus in the next chapter). But that doesn't seem to be the problem with this young man: he's a very likeable young man who's always lived a decent life.

A more radical critique might say that the problem is accumulating wealth, even by apparently legal means. Jesus praises the birds of the air who 'have neither storehouse nor barn' (Luke 12:24). There's a glimpse here of a very radical idea that living in the simplicity of the moment, enjoying the bounties of creation, keeps us closer to God. Accumulating surpluses, hoarding what we don't need, taking it out of circulation, somehow upsets the balance of the created order. Even if I haven't consciously defrauded anyone, my wealth means poverty for somebody else. We're beginning to see the results of that kind of imbalance on a global scale.

But Jesus is also warning of the psychological effects of wealth. Merely having wealth (large or small) can become a trap: it can close our fists around our own little treasures, make us anxious and self-centred instead of generous and open-hearted. Surpluses are meant to be shared (1 Timothy 6:6–10). There's something deeply wrong with a church – or a society – that focuses on 'wealth creation' at the expense of sharing the surplus so that nobody goes short. Better to get rid of it altogether than to find yourself trapped (v. 22). So, the rich man who has everything goes away empty-handed (v. 23: compare Luke 1:53). Ironically, it's the blind beggar (who has nothing) who sees the truth about Jesus (v. 38) – and finds salvation (v. 42).

5 Of tax-collectors and talents

Luke 19:1–27

They still show you Zacchaeus' tree in the back streets of Jericho, an enormous old sycamore tree, bowed down with age. Zacchaeus brings together two themes from the previous chapter. He's a tax-collector, a publican – so he's despised by the righteous as a 'sinner' (compare 18:11). But he's also filthy rich. Tax-farming was a lucrative business opportunity, a form of privatisation of public services. The Romans sold it off to the highest bidder: provided you raised the taxes and kept the Roman governor quiet, you could skim off the profits for yourself. It's a dirty business, but somebody's got to do it.

Zacchaeus is also (famously) a very little man – a slightly comic figure, ducking and weaving behind the crowd to see Jesus. You get the feeling the crowds are politely but firmly crowding him out, pretending he isn't there. But Jesus knows: Jesus looks up into the tree and invites himself round for tea (v. 5). Just as he heard the blind beggar shouting in the street (18:38), Jesus' compassion reaches out, past the indifference of the crowd, even to an unpopular publican, even to the filthy rich – reaches out to this 'son of Abraham' (v. 9), cowering in the trap he's built for himself. Just by being there, accepting his hospitality, treating him as a child of God, Jesus offers him a way out, a way of salvation (vv. 9–10). And (unlike the rich young man) Zacchaeus responds, publicly offering reparation and restoration. A parable becomes reality.

And by pairing Zacchaeus's story with the parable of the talents, perhaps Luke is offering us a way to think about the proper place of wealth in the economy of the kingdom. Any wealth (or talents, or resources) we have, large or small, is something we are given: it is entrusted to us as stewards, to be used for the Master's purposes. He has left us in charge in his absence, and expects us to use what he has given us, not to hide it away (even with the best intentions). Matthew Henry aptly quotes a saying from 'my lord Bacon' on this parable: money is like manure – good for nothing in the heap, but it must be spread (Matthew Henry's *Commentary* on Matthew 25:14–30). And (as Kenneth Bailey suggests) the analogy also encourages boldness: the Master's assets are to be managed publicly in a way that shows where our allegiances lie.

6 The things that make for peace

Luke 19:28–48

All this time, Jesus has been quietly but steadily going up to Jerusalem (v. 28). Now, as he stands on the crest of the Mount of Olives, looking down that precipitous path (v. 37), the narrative gathers pace. Word has gone ahead: here comes the prophet from Galilee, coming to enter the Holy City. A colt appears from nowhere (was there a pre-arranged signal?). The excited crowd of Galilean pilgrims somehow turns into a ceremonial procession. Keep the noise down, Jesus is warned (v. 39), but nothing can stop them now; this is their kingdom moment.

Jesus' entry into Jerusalem is a key moment in all the gospels, a moment of tragic irony that simultaneously sets out the truth about Jesus for all to see and precipitates the negative reactions that will lead to the cross. It's a key point for understanding both the underlying truth of Jesus' kingship and the manner of his kingship. In the chants of the crowd (v. 38) there's an intriguing echo of the angels' song to the shepherds at Bethlehem (Luke 2:14) – only with a difference. Then, the angels sang of peace on earth and glory in the highest heavens: heaven and earth united in a torrent of joy. But now the crowd sing of peace and glory in heaven: maybe a chill warning that peace on earth is more elusive?

And then (only in Luke), Jesus pauses on the way down the hill to weep over the city laid out before him. (The *Dominus Flevit* chapel marks the spot today.) Luke has already shown us Jesus lamenting over Jerusalem (Luke 13). Now, as the king finally comes to his city, this is a moment of crisis (Greek, *krisis* = judgement), a moment for the city to recognise 'the things that make for peace' (v. 42). Peace is here, on offer now: but there's a choice to be made. Kingdom fervour is exciting, invigorating, easy to get swept up in: within 40 years, the city itself would be engulfed in a tide of popular nationalism and opposition to Rome that would lead to the destruction of the temple (vv. 43–44). The teacher from Galilee has entered Jerusalem with a royal procession. He has taken over the temple and is holding the people 'spellbound' by his teaching (v. 48). What comes next? What would Jesus' way of peace look like? The prophet from Galilee has some questions to answer.

Guidelines

The king has come to his city to receive his kingdom, a kingdom that has to be seized by force (16:16). But who will enter the kingdom with him? Who follows in his train? Who are Jesus' 'kingdom people'?

A noisy and obstreperous old woman who refuses to put up with injustice... a blind beggar... a couple of publicans... a bunch of disciples who seem more concerned with what they have given up than with the king himself... and a crowd of excited children. Not a very promising start!

Go back to the first two chapters of Luke's gospel.

Think about the people who surrounded Jesus' birth (Zechariah and Elizabeth, Mary and Joseph, Simeon and Anna), the people who are 'looking forward to the consolation of Israel' (Luke 2:25).

Reread the so-called Canticles, the Magnificat (Luke 1:46–55), the Benedictus (Luke 1:68–79), the Nunc Dimittis (Luke 2:29–32). How are the prophecies made at Jesus' birth being fulfilled at this point in his ministry?

Who are the 'kingdom people' who are making a difference in your life?

Almighty Father,
whose will is to restore all things
in your beloved Son, the King of all:
govern the hearts and minds of those in authority,
and bring the families of the nations,
divided and torn apart by the ravages of sin,
to be subject to his just and gentle rule; through Jesus Christ our Lord.
Amen.

1 By whose authority?

Luke 20:1–26

The first question is a very natural challenge to Jesus' authority (vv. 1–8). Jesus' popularity is rightly seen as a challenge to the temple authorities who have assumed (with Roman support) control of the nation and its spiritual inheritance. Behind it is a question about the interpretation of the scriptures, which all the competing parties claim as the basis for their teaching. Jesus responds with a question of his own: where did John the Baptist get his prophetic authority from? The people instinctively recognised the innate spiritual authority of John's message: he spoke as a prophetic voice from God (compare Luke 3:1–2). But the priestly authorities never recognised this – it was too much of a challenge to their own position.

The parable of the vineyard (vv. 9–18) spells out a deeper answer. To Jesus' audience, the vineyard is a well-known biblical analogy for Israel's covenant relationship with God (compare Isaiah 5). God expects his vineyard to bring forth the fruits of righteousness – both in personal holiness and in just dealings with one another. If there is no fruit, the vineyard is not fit for purpose. Jesus makes a small but significant alteration to the parable. There's nothing fundamentally wrong with the vineyard. It's the management that's the problem – the tenants who have taken on the franchise (as we might say) are refusing to pay the owner his share of the harvest in rent. Things go from bad to worse as the owner's agents are sent away empty-handed, and are finally beaten and shamefully mistreated. What can the owner do?

As Bailey points out, the owner's predicament would be very familiar in a Middle Eastern setting: the owner has been insulted and would be honour-bound to retaliate with anger. But the story takes an unexpected turn. In an extraordinary reversal of cultural expectations, the owner chooses to 'reprocess his anger into grace' (p. 417). He takes the costly path of total vulnerability in sending his beloved son, alone and unarmed, to confront the men who had attacked and humiliated his servants. He hopes that this act of naked trust will awaken the tenants' sense of honour and remind them of what they owe to the vineyard's rightful owner (v. 13). But if they fail to recognise the rightful authority of the owner's son (v. 15), they will ultimately be deprived of the inheritance they were planning to usurp (v. 14).

2 Resurrection questions

Questions, questions! Jesus is challenging old ways of thinking – about scripture; about the kingdom; about the deeper principles that govern the life of the kingdom within the institutions of civil society.

The question of paying taxes to Caesar (vv. 20–26) was a flashpoint in first-century Judea. Popular opposition to the hated poll-tax drew many Judeans into revolutionary dreams of independence from Rome and led eventually to the outbreak of war in AD66. Jesus' answer neatly side-steps the issue and lays down some enduring principles. Paying taxes to fund the benefits of good government is not in itself a problem: every citizen has an obligation to support the systems that maintain civil society (compare Romans 13:1–7). But political allegiances should not compromise the allegiance due only to the living God.

The same goes for our allegiances to marriage and family (vv. 27–40). The ultra-conservative Sadducees accepted only the Torah, the five books of Moses – unlike the Pharisees, who accepted later books such as Daniel, where we find a belief in the resurrection of the dead (Daniel 12:2). Once again, Jesus cuts to the essence of scripture. The Torah itself points to the resurrection. If the basis of eternal life is a relationship with the living God, then the great figures of Israel's past must be alive (Exodus 3:6). It is this fundamental relationship that will define who we are in the world to come – not family, not gender, not country or class (compare Galatians 3:27–29).

In the last of this series of dialogues (vv. 41–44), Jesus raises a question that was fundamental to the early Christian understanding of who Jesus is. The angels at his birth had proclaimed him as Messiah, the Lord's anointed, great David's greater Son. As such, he was the heir of a great tradition, the true fulfilment of ancient Israel's vision of kingship (compare Psalm 72). But then why does David address his own son as 'Lord' (Psalm 110:1)? Here Jesus points ahead to the testimony of the apostolic preachers who used this psalm (one of the most-quoted psalms in the New Testament; compare Acts 2:34–5; Hebrews 1:13; 1 Corinthians 15:25) to tease out the way Jesus' kingship transcends nationalist and human ideas of kingship. Something radically new is breaking in – and yet something in continuity with all that is best in the tradition, with the insights of the great cloud of witnesses down the ages.

3 Wars and insurrections

Luke 21:1–19

Archaeologists have uncovered a graphic record in stone of the war that destroyed the Jerusalem temple in AD70. A marble pavement, hardly worn, lies cracked and buckled by the enormous blocks of masonry toppled down on to it from above. That pavement was part of Herod's massive restoration of the temple: Jesus himself must have walked there. But within 40 years, the temple would become a rebel stronghold in the war against the Romans, stormed by Roman soldiers who gleefully levered off the great stones on to the street below. The sacred vessels were looted and taken to Rome to be paraded in the emperor's triumph. The scene is vividly portrayed on the Arch of Titus, still visible in Rome today as a permanent reminder of the humiliation of Judea. Many of Luke's readers would have seen it.

It has been said that the prophetic vision of the future is like looking at a range of mountains in the distance. On the far horizon, they all merge into one another; but as you get closer, you realise that there are actually several different ranges, with deep valleys between. And often it's the closest that looms the largest. 'When will this be?' (v. 7) sounds like one cataclysmic end-time vision, and indeed, from the perspective of eternity, those who follow Jesus are living in the end-times (v. 32; compare Acts 2:17–21). But Jesus makes it clear that this prophetic vision covers a series of futures, not just one (v. 9). The war with Rome would cause enormous suffering (vv. 20–24), and there would be other wars and natural disasters to follow (v. 10): but 'the end will not follow immediately' (v. 9).

Looking ahead at a world descending into chaos, Jesus is giving his followers something to hang on to. The coming times will test their fortitude to the limit, but they must not succumb to fear (v. 9) or be led astray by deceptive leaders (v. 8). Following Jesus is no guarantee of an easy life: those who seek to follow him will share the vulnerability of the Son of Man (compare 18:31–34). Even within the church, there will be hostility and betrayal (vv. 16–17). See it not as a calamity but as an opportunity to testify, says Jesus (v. 13). Jesus' words and wisdom will live on through the testimony of his followers, not through prepared speeches (v. 14) but through a lifestyle which allows Jesus himself to speak.

4 Landscapes of desolation

Luke 21:20–38

As I write (at the end of 2023), our TV screens are full of images of desolation: destroyed cities, shattered lives, dazed children wandering in the rubble. Jesus' words offer a chilling preview of the ugly brutality of modern warfare, with the total destruction of cities (Mariupol, Gaza), and the so-called 'collateral damage' inflicted on the defenceless, especially women and children (v. 23).

Twice already in this gospel, Jesus has expressed his compassion for the fate of Jerusalem and the suffering of the innocent in time of war (Luke 13:33–35; 19:41–44). The contemporary historian Josephus gives us a vivid description of the Jewish War of AD66–70, ending with a calamitous siege, the rebel leaders holed up in the temple and the city surrounded by Roman armies (v. 20). The final destruction and looting of the temple are a reminder of Daniel's vision of the 'abomination of desolation' (Mark 13:14, citing Daniel 11:31, NKJV). Luke widens out Mark's vision of the desecration of the Holy of Holies to encompass a whole city reduced to desolation (v. 20). In AD70, thousands of Jews were taken captive and sold as slaves after the war, many of them ending up in the slave-markets in Rome. It was a time when it felt as if God's temple and God's worship were being trampled underfoot (v. 24). You can get a sense of how this would feel from some of the Old Testament laments for earlier destructions (compare Psalms 74; 88; the book of Lamentations).

But this is not the end (v. 9)! The destruction of Jerusalem ushers in the 'times of the Gentiles' (v. 24, NKJV), a time of tribulation for all God's faithful people but also a time of fruitful witness (vv. 12–19). The final end-time is still in the future (vv. 25–28): this will be the time of the visible coming of the Son of Man (v. 27; echoes again of Daniel 7). This will not be a little local difficulty: it will be unmistakeable and worldwide (v. 35). This eschatological perspective runs right through the New Testament. However calamitous (or prosperous) our present circumstances, it's never the whole story: we live on the edge of a new world (v. 31). Jesus leaves his disciples with a message both of warning and of hope: warning against taking this world for granted, getting too settled, too comfortable. But also hope: the darkest night comes just before the dawn (v. 28).

5 The upper room

Luke 22:1–27

This is a chapter of preparation: preparation for the Passover; preparation for what lies ahead. Behind the scenes, we see Judas preparing to hand Jesus over to the high priests (vv. 3–6). Luke says nothing about Judas' motivation: what's important is what he does. Up to now, Jesus has been teaching in the temple by day, and retreating to the safety of the Mount of Olives by night. Judas offers a way to break the deadlock by separating Jesus from the protection of the crowds.

But first, Jesus needs to prepare his disciples for what lies ahead. Verses 7–13 focus on the elaborate preparations for the celebration of the Passover – which means entering the city at night, away from the protection of the crowds. Both the time and the place for the feast are laid down in scripture (Deuteronomy 16:6). Passover is a great festival of liberation, looking back to God coming to the rescue of his people when all hope seemed lost (Exodus 14:19–20), and looking *forward* to the future realisation of that liberation in the kingdom of God (vv. 15–18).

But what lies in between? Only Jesus knows what the beloved Son has to do in his own person because nobody else can do it. So, in this last supper discourse, Jesus' focus is on the present significance of this Passover meal. It's a meal to celebrate with your closest family: and Jesus' followers will continue to gather together in fellowship, celebrating God's saving actions in the past and looking forward to the fruition of God's kingdom in the future. But those future gatherings will have a new focus, because the heart of the new covenant, the foundation of God's definitive act of salvation, is Jesus himself. When you break the bread, Jesus says, you are sharing in my body, my life given for you; when you share the wine, you are sharing in my blood, poured out for you as the basis of a new covenant (vv. 19–20).

And then, to crown it all, at this moment of maximum vulnerability, a quarrel breaks out over status (vv. 24–27). Satan really is having a go at Jesus' disciples, just when he needs their support, just when they need to hang together to face what is coming. The only way for Jesus' followers is Jesus' way: the way of the servant King.

6 The Garden of Gethsemane

Luke 22:28–53

The kingdom framework is vital to understanding this farewell discourse. The Bible's view of kingship isn't about entitlement. It's about dispensing justice (vv. 28–30) and upholding the rights of the oppressed (compare Psalm 72). So those who aspire to share Jesus' throne (vv. 24–27) must first learn to follow Jesus' path of identification with the meek of the earth (Isaiah 53:7–9).

And that will mean being tested to the limits (vv. 31–34). All who seek to follow Jesus are potentially vulnerable to attack – especially those in a leadership position. That's how the kingdom of darkness works – by subverting those in a position to influence others. (That's one reason scripture enjoins us to pray for those in power.) All the more reason, therefore, to listen to Jesus (v. 31), to be aware how much we need his prayers – and, when we fall, to repent and come back to receive his forgiveness. Only so can we find the confidence to turn around and strengthen our brothers and sisters (v. 32).

Jesus knows he doesn't have much more time to be with his disciples, at least in this easy, relaxed human way. Isaiah's prophecy about the suffering servant who is 'counted among the lawless' is about to be fulfilled (v. 37; citing Isaiah 53:12). The foundation of the new covenant is that in his beloved Son, God himself is on the side of sinners. But this will mean a fundamental change for the disciples too: their world is about to fall apart and they are totally unprepared for it. So, Jesus reminds them of the time he sent them out on their own (Luke 9—10) and they learned to rely on the hospitality of their neighbours. This time they may not even have that: as associates of a convicted criminal, they will encounter hostility and rejection. Yet even so, when the moment comes, seizing the sword is not what Jesus means: Jesus' touch still brings healing, even in conflict (vv. 47–53).

But first and foremost is the necessity of prayer (vv. 39–46). Jesus goes out into the darkness, as he has done every night, to spend time in prayer in the ancient olive groves of the Garden of Gethsemane, the place where Judas knows he will be. Jesus knows what is coming and knows that its full force will fall on him. The beloved Son knows what the path of obedience demands: but he is also human enough to shrink from what it will mean.

Guidelines

But in the meantime? What does all this do to the way we live in the world? Be alert; watch for the signs of the kingdom; be on guard; pray at all times (21:34–36). These are the basic disciplines of the Christian life – whether the end seems near or far.

This Advent prayer (adapted from Richard Baxter, 1615–91) sums it up well:

Keep us, O Lord,
while we tarry on this earth,
in a serious seeking after you, and in an affectionate walking with you,
every day of our lives;
that when you come,
we may be found not hiding our talent,
nor serving the flesh,
nor yet asleep with our lamp unfurnished,
but waiting and longing for our Lord, our glorious God for ever. Amen.

Our final week of readings will take us through Good Friday and into Easter. Like all the evangelists, Luke slows the narrative down at this point because every moment has significance. If you prefer to keep your readings in step with Holy Week, you might like to read 2:5 and 2:6 on Maundy Thursday, and then re-read 3:1, 3:2 and 3:3 on Good Friday, 3:4 on Holy Saturday, 3:5 on Easter Day and 3:6 on Easter Monday.

1 At the house of Caiaphas

Luke 22:54–71

There is a subtle but important shift in perspective at this point. Through most of the gospel, Jesus is the main actor, always centre-stage. The focus starts to shift now as Jesus is gradually 'handed over' to become the passive object of other people's actions: the anonymous 'they' who seized him and led him away (v. 54). So, we see what happens to Jesus at a distance, through the eyes of other people.

First comes Peter, following at a distance (vv. 54–62), across the Kidron Valley and up the stone steps (which are still there) into the courtyard of the high priest's house. Brave but foolhardy, Peter is caught totally off-guard. The sound of cockcrow (which can still be heard below the church of St Peter in Gallicantu, built over the site of Caiaphas' house) recalls him to a bitter realisation of Jesus' words. But Peter's lowest point is also the beginning of his redemption: Jesus' prayer (v. 32) the memory of Jesus' words (v. 34) and Jesus' piercing glance (v. 61) ensure that there is always a way back.

Where is Jesus meanwhile? All Luke tells us here is that Jesus is casually mocked and humiliated as he waits in custody (vv. 63–65). Jesus' total identification with all who are mocked, shunted around, reduced to passivity by systems of power, is evident here. The irony is that while the soldiers are ridiculing the blindfold Galilean prophet, his prophetic words about Peter are being quietly fulfilled.

Morning comes and, with it, clarity – of a sort. The high-priestly council (vv. 66–71) is looking for evidence to justify laying formal charges before the Roman governor. Caiaphas' question is the key question of Luke's work: is Jesus the Messiah (v. 67)? The quick answer is: Yes, but not as you know it. Jesus refuses to give a one-word response: you have to engage in dialogue with Jesus, to allow him to question you, to work out the real answer. But the clues are there for all to see. Jesus is not only the son of David (20:41–44), the restored king of Israel, but the Son of Man (v. 69), the human figure whom Daniel had seen coming through tribulation to be enthroned 'at the right hand of the power of God' (v. 69: compare Daniel 7:13–14). The final tragic irony is that the chief priests immediately grasp the theological implications of this – but use it to condemn him (v. 71).

2 Pilate and Herod

Jesus is shunted from the council to Pilate to Herod and back again. This series of trials is confusing because they appear to be talking about different things. The priestly council (22:66–71) focuses on theological titles: Messiah as Son of Man and Son of God. As 'Son of Man' (22:69), Jesus will remain in heaven until the time comes for him to return and claim his kingdom (compare Acts 7:55; 1:6–11). But in the trial before Pilate, the charges are framed in political terms: perverting the nation, forbidding taxes, claiming royal status (vv. 2–3). The only kind of Messiah Rome worries about is the kind who might present a political challenge to the empire. Luke is at pains to establish that Jesus was not planning to set up a political kingdom in rivalry to Pilate or Herod. But Jesus' followers will remain in this world, subject to the whims of kings and governors (21:12), so it is important for Luke and his readers that Pilate declares three times, loud and clear, 'I find no basis for an accusation against this man' (v. 4; compare vv. 14–15, 22). Whatever Jesus (and his followers) are up to, it is not a criminal activity.

Herod (vv. 6–12) was Herod Antipas, the wily old fox (Luke 13:32) who had had John the Baptist imprisoned (Luke 3:19–20) and executed. As tetrarch of Galilee, he had no jurisdiction in Judea (which was under direct Roman rule) but was presumably in Jerusalem for the feast of Passover. His presence in Jerusalem gives Pilate another opportunity for passing the buck. It also provides for Luke and his readers yet further evidence of how these apparently random and meaningless events are fulfilling the purposes of God, already revealed in scripture (compare Acts 4:23–28, quoting Psalm 2:1–2).

But none of Pilate's prevarication can prevent the death of an innocent man. John F. Kennedy once said, 'The only thing necessary for the triumph of evil is for good men to do nothing' (attributed to Edmund Burke). When Jesus stands before Pilate, he stands in the place of all victims of injustice, all who are wrongly condemned, all who have no voice or power to establish their innocence. The irony is that in this case he literally dies for – in the place of – a man whose guilt is never in doubt: Barabbas the murderer goes free while Jesus is condemned to death (vv. 18–25).

3 The fellowship of the cross

Luke 23:26–49

Jesus has now definitively crossed the tracks. He is 'numbered among the transgressors' (22:37), labelled as a criminal. Decent people will turn their faces away – or (in a more brutal age) turn up to mock at the spectacle of his execution (vv. 35–37, 48). But there, down among the dregs, he finds surprising pockets of fellowship and shared humanity. Simon of Cyrene (v. 26) is press-ganged into carrying Jesus' cross, sharing the load which Jesus' disciples should have been there to share. Young people from the Syrian Christian church bravely take this role today, carrying the cross through the crowded narrow streets of the old city. Then there are the women of Jerusalem (vv. 27–31), performing one of the few public roles open to women in Jesus' time. To lament is to identify what is wrong at a deep level, to express a profound grief that refuses to be silenced. For Jesus, their lament is a chilling foretaste of the grief and pain that will engulf these streets in a few years' time.

But what is really going on here? The mockery of the bystanders provides a clue. Three times, Jesus is taunted as the one who came to save others and now cannot even save himself (vv. 35–37, 39). The Roman inscription (v. 38) sounds like the ultimate insult. But in fact, as Jesus' words demonstrate, salvation is precisely what is happening here.

First, a word of forgiveness (v. 34), addressed to the Roman soldiers on execution duty. But the soldiers are only obeying orders: there's a bureaucratic labyrinth of complicity in this story. Whose fault was it really? Pilate, who signed the death-warrant? Herod? The chief priests? What about Jesus' disciples, who abandoned him to his fate? 'Father, forgive them,' says Jesus – whoever they are.

Then, a word that reaches beyond death (vv. 39–43). The prisoner's words (v. 42) express the age-old fear of being trapped, sucked into the system, forgotten. Into this situation, Jesus offers his presence, his compassion (literally 'suffering-with'). His words connect our personhood to the person of Jesus: 'Today you shall be with me in paradise' (v. 43). Jesus is the one who remembers and will remember who we are (even when we've forgotten ourselves). Jesus, on the cross, is able to establish relationships that reach beyond death – and win the respect of the centurion (v. 47).

4 The empty tomb

Luke 23:50–56; 24:1–12

Holy Saturday, between Good Friday and Easter Day, is a day of rest, a day of emptiness. The rest of exhaustion, after the emotional roller-coaster of the past 36 hours since Jesus sat down to celebrate the Passover with his disciples. For the passers-by: the end of a spectacle. For the authorities, a job well done, a trouble-maker tidied away. For Jesus' friends, a day of bewilderment and shame: how did this happen? Why didn't I do more? What could I have done?

It was the sabbath – the day of rest (23:56). *Ruht wohl*, sings the choir at the end of Bach's St John Passion: rest in peace. Jesus' final word (23:46) is a word of quiet trust, of surrender into the hands of the Father in words taken from the night-time prayer of Psalm 31, words probably known from childhood. But the sabbath is also a day of completion, the day when God looked at all that he had made and saw that it was good (Genesis 2:1–3). Jesus can rest because his work is completed (John 19:30). Traditional icons of the 'Harrowing of Hell' show a joyful, energetic Saviour bursting the bars of hell, pulling Adam and Eve out of the shadows of death into the light of God's new creation (compare 1 Peter 4:6). 'Love's redeeming work is done: fought the fight, the battle won' (Charles Wesley, 1707–88).

But this sabbath is different: it's become a day of waiting. Not the end of the story, but a day of preparation, opening out into a new, unhoped-for future. Joseph of Arimathea (23:50–54), having watched the council's deliberations and said nothing, decides it's time to take action, to throw in his lot with the victim. At least he can ensure that Jesus' body isn't simply dumped in a communal grave. His action of solidarity unwittingly ensures that the body can be identified: the little group of women, who have followed all the way from Galilee, can mark carefully where he is laid (23:55). Not quite ready to believe, with no idea of what God is going to do, preparing unnecessary spices (23:56–24:1), they still refuse to give up on Jesus, still hold on to the last thing they can do for him. Following their instincts, holding on in the darkness, they become a link in a chain of witnesses, entrusted with the message of the angels (24:5) – even if no one else is ready to believe them.

5 The journey to Emmaus

Luke 24:13–35

In this vivid Easter experience, Luke focuses not on Peter and the eleven, but on two unknown disciples. Luke extends the circle of witness to 'ordinary' disciples (like you and me) – and shows us in the process how Jesus' followers continue to meet him in word and sacrament.

Cleopas and his companion (perhaps his wife?) had been with Jesus on his journey to Jerusalem, sharing the tingling expectation of God's coming kingdom. And then it all fell apart – no kingdom, just a shabby conspiracy and a despicable ending. Had God let them down? Or were they wrong about Jesus all along? You can feel the disappointment – even anger – as we watch them heading home to Emmaus. The stranger, with his gentle, probing questions, gets a sullen response (v. 17). 'What things?' he says (v. 19): and somehow it all pours out. 'We had hoped that he was the one to redeem Israel' (v. 21): that's the point to which Luke's whole story has been pointing. Was it all an illusion? And then there's this weird, unsettling story the women brought back of an empty tomb. A vision of angels? Or a trick of the light?

'But they did not see him' (v. 24). There's the rub: nobody yet in this story has actually seen Jesus. Even though he's walking there beside them, Cleopas and his friend can't see him. What they get instead is a walking Bible study (vv. 25–27), gently but remorselessly peeling away the illusory Messiah they were expecting and showing how everything points to *this* Jesus, the one they had seen dying on the cross, the Messiah who shares the suffering of his people before entering into his glory. Where is God in all this? That's where God is – right at the heart of it. And somehow, frozen hearts begin to warm (v. 32), and the stranger becomes a guest, someone you can't allow to walk out of your life (v. 29).

But it's not until the breaking of the bread – in the simple, familiar actions of taking, blessing, breaking and giving (v. 30) – that their eyes are opened and they are able to see that it was Jesus who had been with them all along. A flash of illumination that sheds light backwards on that long, weary journey ('It was him!') and energises tired legs to go running all the way back to Jerusalem. On this day above all days, Jesus' followers need to be together to celebrate their risen Lord.

6 The road ahead

Luke's gospel ends where it began, in Jerusalem. The story began with Zechariah, the faithful but weary priest of the old covenant, performing his daily duties in the temple – but struck dumb, unable to believe the new story the angel was bringing (1:5–25). It ends with an excited group of Galileans, witnesses to a new covenant, but still gathered in that upper room, still veering between hope and fear, between doubt and joy (vv. 33–35). And then all doubt is at an end: 'Jesus himself stood among them' (v. 36). Beyond hope, beyond doubt, real and tangible, flesh and bone, real enough to share a bit of fish (vv. 42–44).

But this isn't about going back. That old life of walking the roads of Galilee with Jesus, sharing table-fellowship with him – that would be theirs for a few more days (Acts 1:3–4), but not for long. The old life was over: a new world was beginning. So, the final scene of Luke's gospel points forward into the new world of Acts – and opens out into our world.

Our world is one in which Jesus is no longer physically present – but all his followers (not just the apostles!) are called to be his witnesses (v. 48). All that Jesus said and did (Acts 1:1) is important: it's a story that needs to be told (Acts 1:21–22). And that story must incorporate all the disciples' misunderstandings, all their dawning realisation of the true nature of Jesus' kingship, the suffering as well as the rising from the dead (v. 46). It is a world, therefore, in which it will be more important than ever to understand the scriptures, to let go of our illusions and to understand the true nature of the kingdom they point to (vv. 45–46).

It is a world in which the story of Jesus will go on being told and will go on being a good news story of repentance and forgiveness – not just for the people of the old covenant but for all the nations of the world (v. 47: compare Acts 10:34–48). And it's a world in which Jesus' followers will experience his living presence in a new way through the gift of the Holy Spirit (v. 49).

Luke's first volume ends here, with Jesus blessing his disciples as he is carried up to heaven, and his disciples filling the temple with unfettered joy (vv. 52–53). But the story of Jesus' Easter life is only just beginning. Now read on!

Guidelines

Some years ago, I had the privilege of joining a diocesan pilgrimage to the Holy Land. One of many unforgettable days that sticks in my mind is the trip through the upper Jordan Valley to Mount Hermon and the Golan Heights. As the coach climbed the valley, we saw storks wheeling overhead on their migration route from Africa to the coasts of Europe. We saw the ruined palace of Philip the Tetrarch (the brother of the Herod Antipas of the gospels) at Caesarea Philippi. We marvelled at the natural grotto of Banyas in the heart of Hermon, adorned with the relics of pagan devotion – probably where Jesus asked his disciples, 'Who do you say that I am?'. The clear, cold waters of the Jordan gushing out from the rocky caves of Hermon reminded us of Jesus' baptism (and of the 'waves and billows' of Psalm 42). And then we travelled on, to a Druze village up in the mountains and then up to the Golan Heights with their concrete bunkers – which brought us back with a bump to the modern world. From the heights, the view was disconcerting: not the mountain vistas I expected, but a bleak, featureless plain stretching out into the distance – and a signpost announcing that Damascus was only 50 km away.

That view brought home to me the narrow physical and political constraints of the land where Jesus walked. It was a reminder of how close you always are, in this little land, to the wider world and its conflicts – both in Jesus' time and today. And it brought me back to earth from the mountain heights of Mount Hermon to the humdrum vistas of everyday living, from the end of Luke's gospel (if you like) to the beginning of Acts. Easter is always a high point in the Christian year, a great outburst of joy and praise after the tensions and trials of Lent and Holy Week. But Luke's two-volume work doesn't allow us to stop there, up on the mountain-top bathed in the clear light of heaven. Jesus' ascension is not the end but the mid-point of Luke's two-volume work: it's the point from which Luke invites us to follow the disciples down from Jerusalem and out into the world, down through the conflicts and confusions, the triumphs and the disasters, seeking to live as Jesus' witnesses in the world. What makes the difference (to them and to us) is the knowledge of Jesus' living presence warming our hearts as we walk the road, revealing himself to us in the words of scripture and in the breaking of the bread.

And in that light of life I'll walk
Till travelling days are done.

HORATIUS BONAR (1808–89)

FURTHER READING

Loveday Alexander, *People's Bible Commentary: A Bible commentary for every day – Acts* (Centenary classic version) (BRF Ministries, 2022).

Kenneth E. Bailey, *Jesus Through Middle Eastern Eyes* (SPCK, 2008).

Joel Green, *The Gospel of Luke* (New International Commentary on the New Testament) (Eerdmans, 1997)

David Gooding, *According to Luke* (IVP/Eerdmans, 1987).

Matthew Henry's Commentary (one volume: Zondervan, 1960). Widely available online.

Luke Timothy Johnson, *Sacra Pagina: The gospel of Luke* (Liturgical Press, 1991).

Josephus' account of *The Jewish War* is readily available in English: try Mary Smallwood (Penguin Classics, 1981); or Martin Goodman (Oxford World's Classics, 2017).

Multifaith engagement

Andrew Smith

Life in the UK is changing fast, and one area where we see that is in the way that people of different faiths are engaging across society. Whether that's TV chef Nadia Hussain, ex-Prime Minister Rishi Sunak, Mayor of London Sajid Khan, one of Liverpool's top players Mo Salah or the increasing number of communal iftars in public spaces such as Trafalgar Square, The British Museum, various football grounds and even cathedrals. In all our cities, mosques, gurdwaras and mandirs are a feature of the skyline, with some very large and high-profile ones such as the Eco Mosque in Cambridge. We see lights go up in towns to celebrate Diwali and Eid, and many media outlets acknowledging different festivals and experiences of people from all faiths.

This is a marked contrast to the early 2000s, when many people from different faiths, especially Muslims, felt under suspicion because of 9/11 and 7/7, when their experiences and faiths were largely ignored in the media and when it was very rare to see a Muslim woman in a headscarf in the public eye, such as reading the news. Finally, the 2021 census showed increases in the numbers of those following other faiths, especially Islam, while the numbers of those identifying as Christians continues to be in decline.

This presents new questions for Christians as we come to terms with this new reality. How should we respond to life in a country where it is normal to see Muslims, Hindus or Sikhs on TV, where iftar meals are big and sometimes seem to get more exposure than Christian events?

Unless otherwise stated, Bible quotations are taken from NIV.

1 What does the Lord ask of you?

Deuteronomy 10:12–21

Deuteronomy starts with Moses' sermon as the people of Israel stand on the threshold of entering the promised land. The sermon is part recalling all that God has done for them, and part instruction for the future, with repeated emphasis on their need to love God and follow his commands.

Having outlined what God has done and what is going to happen, the sermon takes a significant turn in verse 12. It starts with a rhetorical question, 'And now, Israel, what does the Lord your God ask of you?' – the answer being, to obey, love and serve him. As they enter a new land, where they will encounter different people and the power dynamics will shift, their focus must remain on God. Moses goes on to give a radical view of God's perspective which highlights his power and authority, yet this is held in tension with his justice and compassion. In verse 17, Moses moves seamlessly from describing God as mighty and awesome to God as impartial and incorruptible.

Verse 18 builds on this, describing his care for the fatherless and the widow, but significantly God is described as loving the foreigner who will live among the Israelites. It is because of his love that the Israelites are in turn commanded to love the foreigners who live among them. This is a radical inclusion of people who weren't Jewish, with no suggestion that they have to change their beliefs or behaviours; the impetus is on the Israelites to love them. But the very next verse returns to the command that they are to fear God and serve only him. Love for the foreigner goes hand in hand with love for God, a foreshadowing of the great commandment and a tone that is set to continue throughout scripture.

This joint command gets to the heart of how we are called to live in a country with people of different faiths who are increasingly visible in our neighbourhoods and in the media. Our call is to love them unconditionally and, simultaneously, hold fast to God, to be loving, confident disciples of Jesus Christ. The two commands aren't just different sides of the same coin, separate but joined; rather, they are like two strands woven together as one cord. As we grow in one, we will grow in the other. Loving people of different faiths becomes an intrinsic part of discipleship, drawing us closer to God.

2 Leading well, staying true

Deuteronomy 13

This passage is one that feels very hard to modern ears, with its calls for the death penalty for those seeking to lead the Israelite to worship other gods, evidently something we would never countenance today. The writer is concerned about three types of people who might lead the Israelites astray: those who have the appearance of a spiritual leader (v. 1); those close to home attracted by the gods of other nations (v. 6); and troublemakers who have led a whole town to worship other gods (vv. 12–13). All are to be resisted. The clear message to the people is spelled out in verses 3 and 4: they are to love God and hold fast to him. The writer describes this as a test – will they always follow God? There was a deep concern that living near people of different faiths would tempt them to turn away from God, that the worship and beliefs of others would seem more attractive or easier than holding fast to the Lord's commands. It is important to note that this passage does not condemn those of different faiths; it is those from within the community leading others astray who face judgement.

This is a concern for many Christians in the UK today. Is the presence of different faiths too tempting for some people, drawing them away from following Jesus? There are those who have stopped following Jesus and converted to other religions, which can be deeply unsettling for other Christians. In this context, what should we do, given that yesterday we looked at God's command to love those who are different to us? Invitations to the festivals or celebrations of others, such as iftar meals during Ramadan, is becoming more common and is likely to increase in the coming years. I regularly visit different places of worship, often when their ceremonies are taking place, and usually take other Christians with me. We look to keep our focus on Jesus, while being able to learn about and even appreciate their ceremonies. This is possible but requires us to ensure we return to scripture and prayer, staying rooted in Jesus. The call we have is to stay strong in our faith – the command is to us, not to others. Will we always love God in the midst of an multifaith society?

3 Hear their prayers, O Lord

1 Kings 8:22–43

Imagine the scene: the great new temple, planned for years, is finally completed. It is decorated to God's design by the greatest craftsmen. Holy and sacred items are placed inside, including the ark of the covenant, and the glory of the Lord is so profound and tangible that the priests can't go on with their carefully ordered service. In front of the gathered crowds, the king prays for the dedication of the temple.

If you have never read this dedication prayer in its entirety, it is worth taking the time to and notice Solomon's focus. Amazingly, he starts by declaring that God is so mighty that he cannot dwell in anything as small as this temple (v. 27). The rest of the prayer is taken up by asking God to hear, and answer, the prayers of those who come to the temple. Solomon names the people and times when people might come: those in conflict, when Israel has been defeated, in times of drought, plague or famine, those seeking forgiveness, those seeking or celebrating Israel's victory against her enemies.

So far, so predictable: all the kinds of prayers one could image at such a significant event in the life of the nation. Yet in the middle of this great prayer, Solomon turns his attention outwards to foreigners who might come to pray at the temple (vv. 41–43). First, he is confident that the reason they will come is because they have heard of the mighty deeds of the Lord. Then, outrageously, he asks that God hear their prayer and do whatever they ask. One can imagine some raised eyebrows in the crowd. He hasn't said, 'When they convert' or, 'If they ask things pleasing to you'; he just expresses a desire for God to hear them and do whatever they ask.

That is an incredible act of inclusion and generosity: all people were welcome to come and pray with the hope of an answer. In our cities in the UK, many clergy will tell of how people of all faiths come in to pray, usually quietly on their own. Can we see the prayer of Solomon being answered in small ways in many thousands of churches? And can we also pray, 'Hear them and do whatever they ask'?

4 Small acts of faithfulness

Daniel 1

This opening chapter of Daniel has been preached on and written about many thousands of times. We may know of Daniel and his friends' desire to be faithful to God by refusing to eat the food and wine provided by the king of Babylon and how this led to them being healthier and wiser than all the other students, magicians and enchanters in the kingdom.

Daniel and his friends found themselves in a place where the beliefs and practices of a different religion were dominant. They were a tiny religious minority working out what it meant to be faithful to God in this new context, one where they could no longer rely on old certainties or ways of being. They could look back, wistfully, to the glory days of David and Solomon, but that was not their reality; theirs was one of the ascendancy of others. Throughout the book we read of their desire to be faithful to God in their words and actions, despite the many challenges they faced. Yet the dramatic stories of lions and furnaces were not where they started; their faithfulness to God started in the school of the king, in the seemingly innocuous act of refusing certain foods. Faithfulness to God is rarely dramatic and life-threatening. It usually boils down to simple everyday decisions.

Their faithfulness to God did not lead them to a disdain or arrogance towards the beliefs of the Babylonians; they refused the food, not the instruction in the language and literature of the Babylonians. Throughout the subsequent dramatic stories of their testing, never do they criticise or ridicule the other magicians or seers; as God answers their prayers, so the others are seen to fall short, but it is through God's activity, not the words of Daniel and his companions.

However we choose to read Daniel, as history or allegory of Israel's suffering, it is notable that the writer highlights the corruption of the kings and the faithfulness and power of God. It is a way of living that is consistent with the messages we've already seen; they did not insult their Babylonian captors' beliefs or teachings. What they did was stay faithful to God in the small and the big decisions, underpinning everything with prayer – an example as relevant today as it was then.

5 Living peacefully

Jeremiah 29:1–14

For many people, the world seems bewildering and unlike the place where they grew up, whether that's the changing influence of technology, the climate crisis, changing social attitudes towards sexuality and identity or the growing number and influence of people of different faiths across Britain. Some Christians feel an affinity with the (paraphrased) words of Psalm 137, 'How do we sing the Lord's song in a strange land?' Those words were sung by the Israelites in exile and today's passage is a letter from Jeremiah to them, in a sense answering that question. His letter might have come as a surprise to some, and as a relief for others. He did not call for them to follow the example of Daniel and his friends, standing up to the Babylonian leaders and facing persecution, but rather to be at peace in the land.

First, he states that this is the place to which God carried them (vv. 1, 7). They are not there by accident or because the world is out of control, despite how it might feel. The call in this letter is remarkably relaxed and the instructions are simple to the point of banality: settle down, plant gardens, get married, have children – all just normal life. In the face of great uncertainty and threat, this brings a sense of control and order into life, something that people crave when everything seems out of control. God is saying, 'Be at peace because I am with you. I have not abandoned you, even though you feel insignificant and others have all the power and influence.' Sometimes we need reassurance that we can get on with life; we are not victims of events outside our control. We are in the place God wants us to be.

Second, he instructs them to seek the peace and prosperity of the city. This will benefit them, but it will also help the Babylonians, people of a different culture and faith and the people who have brought them into exile in the first place. This might seem like another obvious command, but for some it would be controversial. Surely, they should seek to undermine the power of others, to wrest back control? We, of course, live in a country where we can influence and change those in power, but do we use our voice and votes just for our benefit or for the good of our local area or country? Do we use it for others' good, even if that means that those of different faiths also benefit, perhaps more than we do?

6 Wisdom from others

What does God do when people of different faiths pray? When a Muslim parent cries out for their child to be healed or a Hindu prays for good health, does God ignore their prayers or respond? This is the conundrum at the heart of Jonah 4. Jonah knew that God would forgive the Ninevites, but he didn't want God to show that grace towards them. Throughout the book, we see Jonah trying to avoid God's command to go and preach to the Ninevites. He flees to Tarshish, and when he eventually gets to Nineveh, his preaching in 3:4 is decidedly thin on detail and forgiveness. In modern language, what we are seeing is his deep-seated prejudice against the Ninevites. He wants to keep God's compassion and forgiveness exclusively for the people of Israel, and in Jonah's eyes, it is not for others. Ironically, it is the king of Nineveh who instructs his people to seek forgiveness from God – with success. God hears their prayers and answers.

In the context of multifaith Britain, this passage is a real challenge to our ideas of God's compassion for those outside the church. How often do we want to claim that his love is just for us, that it is only Christians who can receive his forgiveness? How easy is it to feel jealous or resentful when we see other faiths seeming to do well financially, numerically or politically? Surely that should be us. If we were with Jonah sitting under that tree, what would we say to him? Would we challenge his prejudice or sympathise with his complaint?

The book ends with no easy answer. Jonah is left full of resentment and we don't know how he responds to God's question in verses 10–11. This whole book challenges notions that God's love is only for those inside the Judeo-Christian context. There is no indication that the Ninevites converted to Judaism or had a full understanding of the God to whom they were praying, yet when they cried out, God heard and answered. Can we rejoice if the prayers of those from different faiths seem to be answered, or do we, like Jonah, harbour frustration that God blesses those outside our faith?

Guidelines

These passages have challenged us to see the presence of different faiths through God's eyes. They haven't condoned the beliefs or practices but have seen them as people made in the image of God and loved by him. They remind us that most of the Bible was written in a multifaith context and what we experience now is very familiar. They provoke different emotions in people, both then and now and not always positive, as we saw with Jonah.

- Take some time to reflect on your response to seeing the growth of different faiths in the UK. How do you see that playing out nationally and locally? How does that make you feel? What do you think God is saying to you and to the church in this changing context?

- What would it mean for you to love your neighbours of different faiths? How could you demonstrate this practically? Sending cards at Eid or Diwali, visiting places of worship when offered the chance and attending an iftar meal are all good examples of how we can start to do this.

- If you don't live in an area where there are people of different faiths, how can you still show a love for those who live in the UK? How do you speak about this issue or challenge negative attitudes if you hear them?

- We've looked at passages which show God's love and compassion for those outside the narrow limits of Israel. How does that sit with you? Spend some time thinking about people you know, or see in the media, who are from different faiths. Use these passages to inform your prayers for them, praying for their peace, forgiveness and for God to hear and answer their prayers. Does this change the way you pray?

- How do we seek the peace of the place where we live? What does this mean for our engagement in local politics or community issues? How effective are we, as churches, in working for the peace of our whole community?

- Can your church identify issues that are affecting the peace of your community, who are partners outside the church you could work with to improve things, e.g. police, councillors, other places of worship?

1 Blessings for others

Luke 4:14–30

Our second week of readings in the light of living in multifaith Britain picks up the themes of the reading we had from Jonah. It shows how prejudices keep resurfacing and need to be challenged. In this passage, Jesus is welcomed into his 'home synagogue', where he is handed the scroll of Isaiah to read. The people are impressed at his reading; you can almost hear them whispering to one another with surprise and pride at their local boy: 'Isn't this Joseph's son?' (v. 22). Yet after just a few comments, this approval has turned to such hatred that they drive him out of town and attempt to kill him (v. 29). How does a congregation go from approval to hatred so quickly? What on earth does a preacher say that causes such a sudden and violent reaction?

The change came when Jesus reminded the congregation that the blessings spoken about in Isaiah were not, and never had been, exclusively for the people of Israel but were for the whole world. That, in itself, might have shocked the congregation, but then he goes on to point out that at the time lots of people in Israel were hungry and ill, yet were not blessed in the same way.

For the congregation, this was too much. In their view, God's blessing was solely for his own people – Israel – and to suggest otherwise was so offensive that the message and the messenger had to be expunged. I wonder how a message like this would be received in churches today. Are we ready to see God at work in the lives of people outside the church, even when Christians are struggling, or is that message still too hard? The prejudices that led to the rejection of this message have continued and, sadly, are still with us. Yet Jesus continues to challenge the notion that only God's people will be blessed.

It's important to note that this is the story of one synagogue's reaction. This is not an account of how Jews responded to this message, only the people in this place. This is significant as the extrapolation from the particular to the general is what can lead to anti-Semitic readings of passages, labelling all Jews negatively.

2 Daily life in multifaith Britain

Luke 6:27–41

Today's passage might seem an odd one as we are thinking about life in multifaith Britain, but there are some key commands here that speak directly, and powerfully, into our context.

First, the command to love our enemies. Sadly, I do meet Christians who struggle to perceive adherents of other faiths as either friends or neighbours, and enemies is closer to the truth. What does it mean, then, to do good to those we see as a threat and who we think hate us? Very simply, we do good to them, for example we can visit their places of worship, send greetings on their festivals, smile at them in the street. Many years ago, the leaders of a local mosque objected to the work I was doing and spoke against me during Friday prayers. I decided that every time I passed the mosque, I would pray a blessing on them. I don't know what difference that made then, but now I have a really good relationship with the leaders and am always welcomed with open arms.

Which brings us onto the second command, 'Do to others as you would have them do to you' (v. 31). This gives us an excellent check to see how we are treating others. Do you want people to visit your church? Then do to them as you would have them do to you – visit their place of worship. Do you want them to read our scriptures? Then be prepared to read theirs, and so on. It helps us reflect on what we want life to be like for us, and then to use that as the yard stick for how we treat others. I often say that if you want to do evangelism, be evangelised by someone else and think about how it felt, and then work out how you will share the gospel.

Finally, Jesus gives this humorous metaphor about a speck of sawdust in other peoples' eyes and the plank in our own. Dave Andrews in his book *The Jihad of Jesus* (Wipf and Stock, 2015) unpacks this by highlighting how easily we point out what we see as wrong in others' beliefs or behaviours, but how rarely we look to ourselves. He suggests that this honest, humble willingness to confront our own failings is vital before we ever try to correct others. This is deeply challenging, and for some controversial, but takes seriously this teaching and opens up a way of gracious, humble encounters with others.

3 Holding firm in confusing times

John 14:1–14

So far in this series of studies, we've looked at passages that show the wideness of God's mercy. Today we look at a passage that is often used to demonstrate exclusivity in Christian theology that puts other faiths outside of any path to salvation. Engaging with scripture always means grappling with the complexity and breadth of teaching and not just reading passages which confirm views we already hold.

Jesus did not speak these words as a commentary on religious pluralism, but as comfort to his disciples. This chapter follows the unsettling example of Jesus washing their feet, his pronouncement that one of them will betray him and Peter being told he will deny Jesus. No wonder the chapter starts with Jesus saying, 'Do not let your hearts be troubled' (v. 1). It then goes on to focus the disciples' security and comfort of knowing the Father, which Jesus says is through him. Some pluralist theologians point out that he doesn't say, 'I am the only way', so he can be considered 'the way' in the same way that two roads go from one town to another; they are both the way, but not the only way. The traditional interpretation is that Jesus meant he is the only way to the Father, suggesting an exclusivity that does not sit well with contemporary views that all religions are paths to God.

The Bible holds this tension of God's love for the world alongside working out this love through a specific group of people – Israel, or though the exclusive life of Jesus. This can make us sound arrogant or dismissive of others, but both those attitudes contradict Jesus' teachings of how we should live; believing Jesus is the only way to the Father does not override commands to love our neighbour, be a servant, walk humbly with God, etc. This passage calls the disciples to hold on to their faith in Jesus, knowing that he will lead them to the Father. In a world of competing truth claims and diverse spiritualities, this is a vital call to the church – be strong followers of Jesus and he will lead you to the Father. We can hold this view and share it lovingly and humbly with others. It should inspire us to care for our neighbours of different faiths, and to show them the love of Christ.

4 Life's a riot

Acts 19:23–41

The riot in Ephesus finds Paul and his companions caught up in conflict with the worshippers of Artemis. In this account, Paul has a minor part, as the two main characters are Demetrius and the city clerk.

Demetrius is a man who, while he opposed the teaching of the gospel, we can understand. He was a man of passionate faith; his way of life and livelihood was focused on the worship of Artemis. However, his faith was fragile, he was concerned that the preaching of the gospel would turn people away from Artemis with the result that he, and his colleagues, would lose their livelihoods.

I encounter many Christians in the UK who are like Demetrius; they see the rise of different faiths and the decline in religious belief and fear that this is the end of the church. They see Jesus being discredited; some fear the loss of the churches influence in politics, education, etc. While this doesn't lead to riots, the language some use is as intemperate and aggressive as Demetrius.

The clerk is also a man of great faith who has none of the anxieties of Demetrius; he is absolutely sure in his belief that the image of Artemis in the temple fell from heaven (vv. 35–36). Because of his confidence, he doesn't need to be afraid; his faith leads him into serious leadership at a time of crisis, even challenging his own community's behaviour.

Perhaps most intriguing is what he says about Paul and his companions (v. 37), that they have neither robbed the temple nor blasphemed the goddess. We wouldn't expect Paul to rob a temple, but how easy would it have been to say things about Artemis that others perceive as blasphemy? Paul was able to preach the gospel in such a way that no one could criticise what he said. It is so easy to be critical of other religions, to have cheap shots at their beliefs, in order to make the gospel look good. This is never necessary, as Paul demonstrated: the gospel is good news on its own terms, not just in comparison to others. Many of us can identify with the anxiety of Demetrius, but it is to the example of the clerk and Paul that we turn, the clerk confident yet gracious, Paul's preaching clear without being insulting.

5 Responding to criticism with integrity

1 Peter 3:8–18

Social media can be a toxic place. It seems to bring out the worst in people and, sadly, religious people are no different. People are quick to make accusations or trade insults, and this fuels similar behaviour in face-to-face contacts as well. While we live in a country where diversity is generally celebrated, this isn't always the case. Sometimes it can feel as if people are happy to criticise religious belief, and as Christians we can experience insults and criticisms. We are, of course, far from unique in this. Most of the New Testament is written against the backdrop of persecution which was far worse than we experience in the UK. We have become used to the fact that the Christian life is lived in comfort, but when we look round the world, we see this is the exception not the rule.

Peter wrote this epistle to Christians who were exiles because of persecution; therefore it is practical advice for holy living with teaching that echoes Luke 6. Peter's instruction is an exhortation to holy living after the example of Jesus, a theme running through the epistle. His challenge is to respond to attacks by being even more Christlike to repay evil with blessing (v. 9) and to keep a clear conscience (v. 16). When they get chance to speak of their faith, he urges his readers to do this (v. 15) and to do so with gentleness and respect.

This passage gives us a clear model for how we live in a society of many different and competing beliefs, world views and lifestyles. First, we should live godly lives; second, we should be doing good; third, we should be ready to (gently and respectfully) give the reason for the hope we have; and finally, we should maintain a clear conscience so that people who want to criticise us are ashamed of their slander.

When encountering people of different faiths who might be critical of Christianity, it is so easy to respond with equal criticism or to keep quiet. We can respond by gently explaining what we believe, but we must also keep a focus on being clear witnesses through our godly lifestyles and good works. How we live among neighbours of other faiths is as important as what we say and how we say it.

6 Love as a way of life

1 Corinthians 12:31—13:13

We conclude this series of readings that speak into life in a multifaith society by looking at another famous passage. While this was originally written to the church in Corinth about how they live together, it is legitimate to see this as an exploration of what it means to love in a broader context. We are called to love our neighbours and our enemies, so however you view people of different faiths, this has something to say about what that love looks like.

First, it is the most excellent way: truth and wisdom are important, but they are as nothing without love. It is so easy to think that proclaiming truth is all that matters, but unless it is done from a place of genuine love, it is just noise, shouting into the void with no positive impact. We can do good, following the exhortation of Peter in yesterday's reading, but if we do it without love it is as nothing. These are tough words, but they open up a way of being that transforms us and our relationships with others. It is tempting to focus solely on truth claims, arguing about the divinity and humanity of Jesus or the trinity, but done without love these words fall on deaf ears. I once heard the former Archbishop of Canterbury Dr Rowan Williams say, 'Jesus didn't die on the cross so that we could win arguments in pubs.' Winning arguments is not what this idea of love is all about.

The passage goes on to list several characteristics of love that serve as an ethical guide to how we should live. This is love lived out in our neighbourhoods: the call to be patient and kind, not to boast about what Christians do or how many there are, not to be jealous of the success of others or keep a record of wrongs that people have done against us. As we work through this list, we can see how it transforms the way we relate to those of different faiths we encounter. It is this example of love that should define our relationship and that will outlast our words and deeds. When we struggle to know what to do or say, when we feel overwhelmed, our greatest calling is to love and let the rest flow from there.

Guidelines

The first Christians lived among people of different faiths, working out what it meant to be followers of Jesus when they faced persecution. The readings have focused on being a minority and seeking to be confident followers of Christ in a religiously plural world.

- Luke 6 is challenging. Reflect on the command, 'do to others as you would have them do to you'. Think through how obeying this might affect the way you speak or act towards people of different faiths.

- Have you ever had someone try to convert you to a different religion or service provider? What did you like about the encounter? What irritated you? What lessons do you learn from this about how to tell people the good news?

- If you shared your faith with someone of a different faith, what imagery or emphasis would you give? Could you sum up what you believe in a few sentences? Would you have said anything that they considered blasphemous or critical of their religion? Think through how you describe the gospel making sure you remove any criticisms of others.

- There is a focus in these passages on living a holy life in the midst of different faiths and criticism. Spend some time praying through your own lifestyle, committing or re-committing your speech, thoughts and behaviour to Christ. Ask for forgiveness for those areas where you don't get it right, knowing that forgiveness always follows genuine repentance.

- Worshipping Jesus Christ should never lead to arrogance. Read through the 1 Corinthians 12 passage again, reflecting on what those words mean for how we love the people of different faiths living in the UK.

FURTHER READING

Ray Gaston, *Faith, Hope and Love: Interfaith engagement as practical theology* (SCM, 2017).

Ida Glaser, *The Bible and Other Faiths: What does the Lord require of us?* (Langham Global Library, 2012).

Andrew Smith, *Vibrant Christianity in Multifaith Britain* (BRF Ministries, 2018).

Richard Sudworth, *Distinctly Welcoming: Christian presence in a multifaith society* (Scripture Union, 2007).

SHARING OUR VISION – MAKING A GIFT

I would like to make a donation to support BRF Ministries.
Please use my gift for:

☐ Where it is most needed   ☐ Anna Chaplaincy   ☐ Living Faith
☐ Messy Church   ☐ Parenting for Faith

Title	First name/initials	Surname
Address		
		Postcode
Email		
Telephone		
Signature		Date

Please accept my gift of:

☐ £2 ☐ £5 ☐ £10 ☐ £20 Other £ [   ]

by (delete as appropriate):

☐ Cheque/Charity Voucher payable to 'BRF'

☐ MasterCard/Visa/Debit card/Charity card

Name on card

Card no. [   ] [   ] [   ] [   ]

Expires end [M][M] [Y][Y]   Security code* [   ]   *Last 3 digits on the reverse of the card

Signature	Date

Please complete other side of form

BRF Ministries Gift Aid Declaration

In order to Gift Aid your donation, you must tick the box below.

☐ I want to Gift Aid my donation and any donation I make in the future or have made in the past four years to BRF Ministries

I am a UK taxpayer and understand that if I pay less Income Tax and/or Capital Gains Tax in the current tax year than the amount of Gift Aid claimed on all my donations, it is my responsibility to pay any difference.

Please notify BRF Ministries if you want to cancel this Gift Aid declaration, change your name or home address, or no longer pay sufficient tax on your income and/or capital gains.

You can also give online at **brf.org.uk/donate**, which reduces our administration costs, making your donation go further.

Our ministry is only possible because of the generous support of individuals, churches, trusts and gifts in wills.

☐ I would like to leave a gift to BRF Ministries in my will.
Please send me further information.

☐ I would like to find out about giving a regular gift to BRF Ministries.

For help or advice regarding making a gift, please contact our fundraising team +44 (0)1235 462305

Your privacy

We will use your personal data to process this transaction. From time to time we may send you information about the work of BRF Ministries that we think may be of interest to you. Our privacy policy is available at **brf.org.uk/privacy**. Please contact us if you wish to discuss your mailing preferences.

Registered with

(FR)

FUNDRAISING
REGULATOR

● Please complete other side of form

Please return this form to 'Freepost BRF'
No other address information or stamp is needed

Bible Reading Fellowship is a charity (233280) and company limited by guarantee (301324), registered in England and Wales

GL0125

Guidelines forthcoming issue

The May issue of *Guidelines* is shaping up well! Here is what you can expect.

We tackle some difficult Old Testament books in this issue. Helen Paynter takes us through the book of Numbers, often maligned as boring or irrelevant, and shows us how it crackles with excitement and depth. Victoria Omotoso helps us examine the book of Lamentations. She argues that the book is a form of protest, as well as a tool for processing the messy emotions of grief, anger and ultimately hope. Finally, Miriam Bier Hinksman guides us through Hosea, another book dealing with complicated emotions and sensitive issues.

In the New Testament, our recurring three-week series begins with Steve Walton, who reflects on Acts 1—9. Helen Miller helps us to understand 1 Corinthians, where we find we are challenged and encouraged by Paul's kind but firm words to a troubled church. Tim Welch takes us through the brief but challenging letter of James, that infamous 'gospel of straw'. Tim helps us to see the pithy wisdom teaching, as well as the breadth of sayings and everyday illustrations that prove accessible and memorable for any age and culture.

As ever, we also offer some themed readings and reflections. George Wieland uses the gospel of Luke to accompany him as he identifies 'teachable moments' for both the disciples and for us today. Tanya Marlow also spends time in the gospels looking specifically at the healing miracles from a disability perspective. Valerie Hobbs, meanwhile, examines the theme of war and peace as she exposes the absurdity of war and its roots in greed and arrogance, before focusing on the grief and restlessness that all earthly empires inflict, in tension with the hope for peace and justice God offers us both today and in the life to come. Finally, Johannes J. Knecht looks at six female images for God in the Old Testament, and explores the fact that scripture applies both male and female creaturely pictures to elucidate something of the beauty of God.

Thank you to those who have written in to provide feedback. We value hearing what our readers have to say, so do let us know if you have particularly enjoyed – or particularly struggled with – any theme, topic or argument. We'd love to hear from you. To send feedback, please email **enquiries@brf.org. uk**, phone **+44 (0)1865 319700** or write to **BRF Ministries, 15 The Chambers, Vineyard, Abingdon OX14 3FE**.

What the Bible means to me: Max Kramer

 I'm someone who discovered the Bible at university – almost accidentally. I'd always sung at school and discovered that the most straightforward way of singing post-18 was to join the chapel choir. I was simply there for the music – or at least I thought I was. Sitting through the rest of the service politely was just the price I was willing to pay to continue my childhood hobby.

But, slowly, hearing the Bible read and interpreted began to exercise an attraction that led, first, to my baptism and confirmation, and then to my exploration of ordination.

The nature of that attraction was and is important to me. It wasn't as if I was sitting in one place, and I slowly became convinced of the truth of some other set of beliefs that were at some remove from my life. Rather, the more I heard of the Bible the more I realised these stories resonated with my own experience. They 'nailed' experiences I had had, or people I had known, or features of our society and our world. They articulated for me the stuff that was at the heart of my own world and the world I shared with others.

Just one example: in Matthew 20, Jesus tells a story about a vineyard. You probably know it well. The owner hires workers in the morning and offers them one denarius' pay, and then hires others at noon, and then twice in the afternoon. When the hour for payment comes and all are paid the same, the workers hired in the morning complain. It isn't fair. How can they get the same for working just a few hours when we have been at it all day? But the owner reminds them of his original deal and asks, 'Are you envious because I am generous?'

Isn't that just spot on about how we human beings are? We care so much less about the good things we have than about the fact we don't have as much as someone else. Or that we work so hard and someone else seems to get away with coasting, or just with being lucky – in life, in work, in the church. The Bible just *gets* what it is to be truly human and through this insight and honesty helps us to understand our place in this God-created world.

The scriptures, then, are texts that always open things up. They open our eyes to see our own lives in a deeper and richer way, constantly revealing ever new insights into the business of becoming more human and more 'divine,' two journeys which are inseparably related.

For me, God's gift of the scriptures is his poetic complement to his raw gift of my life. The Bible doesn't stand over and against me with 'I want X but the Bible says Y,' but it's a text, or, better, an experience, that provides the interface in which, and through which, and sometimes even against which, I can discover who I am becoming, what I truly want and what really matters in relationship with others and with God.

Recommended reading

There is no doubt that each of us has a place in the Easter story, but what happened on the cross is not just a story of me and Jesus. It is far deeper and wider than that.

In *The Whole Easter Story*, BRF Ministries' 2025 Lent book, Jo Swinney explores the broader impact of the Easter story on God's relationship with creation. Through Bible readings, reflections and stories from A Rocha's global conservation efforts (including illustrations of species they work to support), discover how the cross transforms not just our own individual connection with Jesus, but also our relationships with each other and our world.

The following is an edited extract taken from the reading for Day 1. Entitled 'Created', it is a reflection on Psalm 139:13–16.

I have twice had the strange experience of growing a human in my body. At first the only evidence of their existence was a pink line on a plastic stick. After a few weeks they made me feel very sick, and then they grew big enough to give me a bump and a great deal of discomfort. When I look at my teenage daughters, I find it hard to connect these beautiful, fully grown, and increasingly independent people with anything that might have gone on inside me. We may have sophisticated scanning equipment now that makes the womb slightly less secret, but I can still relate to the idea that babies develop in 'the depths of the earth', a process shrouded in mystery and deep darkness.

I can also confirm that I was not a consciously active participant in the task of taking Alexa and Charis from being a couple of cells to fully formed babies. It was God who created them, who breathed life into their beings, who gave them their fingerprints, their temperaments, their quirks and tendencies. As humans we have become very clever in certain regards. We know our bodies are composed of eleven elements (oxygen, hydrogen, nitrogen, carbon, calcium, phosphorus, sulphur, potassium, sodium, chlorine, and magnesium, in case you were wondering). But we have no clue how to combine those elements into a living, breathing, emotional and spiritual being.

As we begin to consider our relationship with God in the context of the

Easter story, a good place to start is with the fact he is creator, and we are created. We were created as homo sapiens, a distinct species among many, imprinted with the very image of God (Genesis 1:27), and we were each and every one of us created, seen, significant and loved before one of our days came to be.

I have heard the story told from a different starting point, as I imagine you have. Sometimes it is told like this: people are awful; we are dirty, sinful, horrid things, and we took God right to the end of his tether, so he had to come and die for us.

I found a website giving step-by-step instructions for evangelism, and this is step two (step one was about sin too):

> Write the word 'SIN' vertically between the words 'MAN' and 'GOD'. Quote Romans 3:23 – 'For all have sinned and fall short of the glory of God.' Questions to ask: 'What does the word "all" in this verse mean? Does it include you?' Always use questions after giving a verse so that you may know whether its truth is getting across. Say, 'Since God is holy and man is sinful, sin separates man from God.'

But the Bible doesn't start with sin; it starts with creation, and that makes all the difference to how we understand our relationship with God. Let's dig into Psalm 139 and you'll see what I mean.

Psalms are songs reflecting the experience of their authors' lives with God and infused with references to early sections of scripture, books of history, prophecy, poetry and apocalypse. They were written long before the life of Jesus, but in the understanding that all too often humankind was failing, corporately and individually, to keep their side of the covenant promises that framed their relationship with God. King David led his people into so many bloody battles that he was forbidden from building a temple. His relationship history would definitely have earned him a well-deserved 'Love Rat' tabloid splash. He worshipped God with all his heart but sometimes cursed him too. In all this complexity, one thing was clear: as a being created by God, he knew his intrinsic worth was never up for debate – 'Your works are wonderful' (v. 14).

David's language in Psalm 139 describes a very hands-on process of making – he uses words like 'knitted' and 'woven'. These crafts involve patterns, but patterns which allow for creativity. Each human is like others, and at the same time unique. We are wired with a need for significance, to have a place, to be seen and known as an individual, not just a speck in a blurry crowd of billions, and thankfully we have a God with the capacity to relate to each of us – 'Your eyes saw [me]… all the days ordained for me were written in your book' (v. 16). We can base our self-esteem on everything from an annual appraisal at work, to the number of hearts under our Instagram posts, to how many people show up to our birthday drinks, but why would we? Each of us has been 'fearfully and wonderfully made' (v. 14) by our ever-loving creator God.

For reflection

Think about some of the people who have shaped how you see yourself, from parents to teachers, to friends and spouses, to employers and media figures. How much power have you given their voices? How can you let God's voice speak more loudly, and what would change if you decided to listen only to him when it comes to your worth?

Prayer

Abba, Father, I am yours. You meant me to be here, and you look at me with love and pleasure. Your knowledge of me is deeper than I can fathom. My feelings, motivations and impulses are laid bare before you. I can't deceive you; I can't hide from you. Thank you that your commitment to me is unshakeable. Amen.

Salish sucker (*Catostomus sp. cf. catostomus*)

A small freshwater fish thought to be locally extinct – until it was identified in the Little Campbell River watershed (British Columbia, Canada) in 2011! The population is now thriving.

To order a copy of The Whole Easter Story, *use the order form on page 153 or visit* **brfonline.org.uk**

Through revelations ten to sixteen of her *Revelations of Divine Love*, Julian of Norwich returns time and again to the idea that 'all is well', and Emma Pennington examines this popular mantra and explores what Julian really means by it, bringing depth and relevance to these words for the reader who lives in an age of pandemic, war and climate crisis which closely echoes Julian's own. Deep engagement with Julian's visions of salvation encourages the reader to reflect in prayer and devotion on their own personal relationship with God.

All Shall Be Well
Visions of salvation with Julian of Norwich
Emma Pennington
978 1 80039 206 9 £12.99
brfonline.org.uk

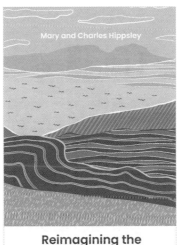

Reimagining the Landscape of Faith
Essential pathways for spiritual growth

Is this all there is to faith? Mary and Charles Hippsley help us to identify our faith map, including the unexamined assumptions that underpin it. Then, drawing on a range of sources of wisdom including personal experience, they gently encourage us to allow God to expand our map when we find that our faith doesn't match up with the reality of life. They aim to equip the reader to navigate their journey towards maturity by exploring new paths and landscapes of faith.

Reimagining the Landscape of Faith
Walking with Jesus through retirement beginnings and endings
Mary and Charles Hippsley
978 1 80039 271 7 £9.99
brfonline.org.uk

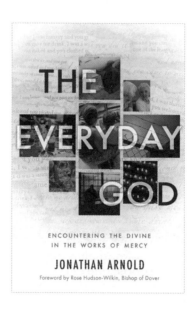

Jonathan Arnold, a seasoned community engagement expert, delves deep into the heart of the biblical mandate to love one's neighbour. Through a tapestry of real-life stories, he unveils the power of practical faith, illustrating how it can ignite transformation among the poor and vulnerable. As he reflects upon Jesus' teaching in Matthew 25:34–40, Arnold challenges us to discover God's presence in the most unexpected places and join in with where he is acting, whether inside or outside our churches.

The Everyday God
Encountering the Divine in the works of mercy
Jonathan Arnold
978 1 80039 210 6 £9.99
brfonline.org.uk

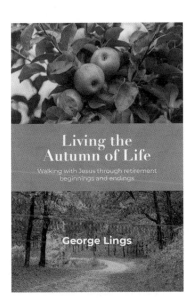

How can we best approach the season between retiring and becoming dependent? Autumn is a time of gains and losses: fruit being harvested, and leaves falling. This book charts the experience of living through both realities, drawn from the author's own life and from the views of interviewees. Informed by historical and contemporary reading, it offers snapshots of later life, taken against a backdrop of ageism in society and church. George Lings reflects on the identity of the 'active elderly', and considers through a biblical lens the challenges and opportunities that this season brings.

Living the Autumn of Life
Walking through retirement beginnings and endings
George Lings
978 1 80039 282 3 £12.99
brfonline.org.uk

'Truly transformative' **PAUL WOOLLEY, CEO, LICC**

Weaving together biblical perspectives with academic research and his own experiences of working in different settings, Chris Gillies lays the theological foundation for work, moves on to examining biblical role models from both Old and New Testaments, and concludes by exploring common issues we wrestle with in our work, from money matters or managing and leading others to knowing if we're in the right job or simply doing the right thing.

On the Way to Work
A Christian approach to thinking differently about success and fulfillment
Chris Gillies

978 1 80039 239 7 £12.99

brfonline.org.uk

To order

Online: **brfonline.org.uk**
Telephone: **+44 (0)1865 319700**
Mon–Fri 9.30–17.00

Delivery times within the UK are normally 15 working days. Prices are correct at the time of going to press but may change without prior notice.

Title	Price	Qty	Total
BRF Lent Book: The Whole Easter Story	£9.99		
All Shall Be Well	£12.99		
Reimagining the Landscape of Faith	£9.99		
The Everyday God	£9.99		
Living the Autumn of Life	£12.99		
On the Way to Work	£12.99		

POSTAGE AND PACKING CHARGES			
Order value	UK	Europe	Rest of world
Under £7.00	£2.00	Available on request	Available on request
£7.00–£29.99	£3.00		
£30.00 and over	FREE		

Total value of books	
Donation*	
Postage and packing	
Total for this order	

Please complete in BLOCK CAPITALS

* Please complete and return the Gift Aid declaration on page 140.

Title .... First name/initials .... Surname ....

Address ....

.... Postcode ....

Acc. No. .... Telephone ....

Email ....

Method of payment

☐ Cheque (made payable to BRF) ☐ MasterCard / Visa

Card no. ☐☐☐☐ ☐☐☐☐ ☐☐☐☐ ☐☐☐☐

Expires end ☐M ☐M ☐Y ☐Y Security code* ☐☐☐ * Last 3 digits on the reverse of the card

We will use your personal data to process this order. From time to time we may send you information about the work of BRF Ministries. Please contact us if you wish to discuss your mailing preferences. brf.org.uk/privacy

Registered with
FUNDRAISING
REGULATOR

Please return this form to:

BRF Ministries, 15 The Chambers, Vineyard, Abingdon OX14 3FE | enquiries@brf.org.uk

For terms and cancellation information, please visit brfonline.org.uk/terms.

Bible Reading Fellowship is a charity (233280) and company limited by guarantee (301324), registered in England and Wales

BRF Ministries needs you!

If you're one of our regular *Guidelines* readers, you will know all about the benefits and blessings of regular Bible study and the value of serious daily notes to guide, inform and challenge you.

Here are some recent comments from *Guidelines* readers:

'… very thoughtful and spiritually helpful. [These notes] are speaking to the church as it is today, and therefore to Christians like us who live in today's world.'

'You have assembled an amazingly diverse group of people and their contributions are most certainly thoughtful.'

If you have similarly positive things to say about *Guidelines*, would you be willing to share your experience with others? Could you ask for a brief slot during church notices or write a short piece for your church magazine or website? Do you belong to groups, formal or informal, academic or professional, where you could share your experience of using *Guidelines* and encourage others to try them?

It doesn't need to be complicated: just answering these three questions in what you say or write will get your message across:

- How do *Guidelines* Bible study notes help you grow in knowledge and faith?
- Where, when and how do you use them?
- What would you say to people who haven't yet tried them?

We can supply further information if you need it and would love to hear about it if you do give a talk or write an article.

For more information:
- Email **enquiries@brf.org.uk**
- Telephone BRF Ministries on +44 (0)1865 319700 Mon–Fri 9.30–17.00
- Write to us at BRF Ministries, 15 The Chambers, Vineyard, Abingdon OX14 3FE

Inspiring people of all ages to grow in Christian faith

At BRF Ministries, we long for people of all ages to grow in faith and understanding of the Bible. That's what all our work as a charity is about.

- Our **Living Faith** range of resources helps Christians go deeper in their understanding of scripture, in prayer and in their walk with God. Our conferences and events bring people together to share this journey, while our Holy Habits resources help whole congregations grow together as disciples of Jesus, living out and sharing their faith.

- We also want to make it easier for local churches to engage effectively in ministry and mission – by helping them bring new families into a growing relationship with God through **Messy Church** or by supporting churches as they nurture the spiritual life of older people through **Anna Chaplaincy**.

- Our **Parenting for Faith** team coaches parents and others to raise God-connected children and teens, and enables churches to fully support them.

Do you share our vision?

Though a significant proportion of BRF Ministries' funding is generated through our charitable activities, we are dependent on the generous support of individuals, churches and charitable trusts.

If you share our vision, would you help us to enable even more people of all ages to grow in faith? Your prayers and financial support are vital for the work that we do. You could:

- Support BRF Ministries with a regular donation;
- Support us with a one-off gift;
- Consider leaving a gift to BRF Ministries in your will (see page 156);
- Encourage your church to support BRF Ministries as part of your church's giving to home mission – perhaps focusing on a specific ministry;
- Most important of all, support BRF Ministries with your prayers.

Donate at **brf.org.uk/donate** or use the form on pages 139–40.

God is in control

Then Job answered the Lord: 'I know that you can do all things and that no purpose of yours can be thwarted.'

JOB 42:1–2 (NRSV)

We sometimes forget the more cheerful ending of the book of Job. As we have continued to live through challenging times, be that on personal, national and international levels, the reminder that God has it all under control is a reassuring promise to hold on to.

In this season, the Living Faith team are providing materials for Lent and Easter, and our collection of Easter and everyday cards is growing. Meanwhile, resources for Advent and Christmas are being prepared.

The Anna Chaplaincy, Messy Church and Parenting for Faith teams continue to offer training, resources and events supporting individuals and churches with their invaluable work, which really does enable people to grow in Christian faith across all ages and to know God cannot be thwarted.

We believe this work is invaluable, and we are assured of this by the kind feedback we receive. However, none of this would be possible without kind donations from individuals, churches charitable trusts and gifts in wills. If you would like to support us now and in the future you can become a Friend of BRF Ministries by making a monthly gift of £2 a month or more – we thank you for your friendship.

Find out more at **brf.org.uk/donate** or get in touch with us on **01235 462305** or via **giving@brf.org.uk**.

We thank you for your support and your prayers.

The fundraising team at BRF Ministries

> Give. Pray. Get involved.
> **brf.org.uk**

GUIDELINES SUBSCRIPTION RATES

Please note our new subscription rates, current until 30 April 2026:

Individual subscriptions
covering 3 issues for under 5 copies, payable in advance
(including postage & packing):

	UK	Europe	Rest of world
Guidelines 1-year subscription	£21.30	£29.55	£35.25
Guidelines 3-year subscription (9 issues)	£60.30	N/A	N/A

Group subscriptions
covering 3 issues for 5 copies or more, sent to one UK address (post free):

Guidelines 1-year subscription £15.75 per set of 3 issues p.a.

Please note that the annual billing period for group subscriptions runs from 1 May to 30 April.

Overseas group subscription rates
Available on request. Please email **enquiries@brf.org.uk**.

Copies may also be obtained from Christian bookshops:

Guidelines £5.25 per copy

All our Bible reading notes can be ordered online
by visiting **brfonline.org.uk/subscriptions**

GUIDELINES INDIVIDUAL SUBSCRIPTION FORM

To set up a reoccurring subscription, please go to
brfonline.org.uk/gl-subscription

Title .... First name/initials .... Surname ....

Address ....

.... Postcode ....

Telephone .... Email ....

Please send *Guidelines* beginning with the May 2025 / September 2025 /
January 2026 issue (*delete as appropriate*):

(*please tick box*)	UK	Europe	Rest of world
Guidelines 1-year subscription	☐ £21.30	☐ £29.55	☐ £35.25
Guidelines 3-year subscription	☐ £60.30	N/A	N/A

Optional donation to support the work of BRF Ministries £ ....

Total enclosed £ .... (cheques should be made payable to 'BRF')

Please complete and return the Gift Aid declaration on page 140 to make your
donation even more valuable to us.

Please charge my MasterCard / Visa with £ ....

Card no. ☐☐☐☐ ☐☐☐☐ ☐☐☐☐ ☐☐☐☐

Expires end [M][M] [Y][Y] Security code ☐☐☐ Last 3 digits on the reverse of the card

We will use your personal data to process this order. From time to time we may send you
information about the work of BRF Ministries. Please contact us if you wish to discuss your mailing
preferences **brf.org.uk/privacy**

Please return this form with the appropriate payment to:
BRF Ministries, 15 The Chambers, Vineyard, Abingdon OX14 3FE
For terms and cancellation information, please visit **brfonline.org.uk/terms**.

Bible Reading Fellowship is a charity (233280) and company limited by guarantee (301324),
registered in England and Wales

GL0125

GUIDELINES GIFT SUBSCRIPTION FORM

☐ I would like to give a gift subscription (please provide both names and addresses):

Title .... First name/initials .... Surname ....

Address ....

.... Postcode ....

Telephone .... Email ....

Gift subscription name ....

Gift subscription address ....

.... Postcode ....

Gift message (20 words max. or include your own gift card):

....

....

Please send *Guidelines* beginning with the May 2025 / September 2025 / January 2026 issue *(delete as appropriate)*:

(please tick box)	UK	Europe	Rest of world
Guidelines 1-year subscription	☐ £21.30	☐ £29.55	☐ £35.25
Guidelines 3-year subscription	☐ £60.30	N/A	N/A

Optional donation to support the work of BRF Ministries £ ....

Total enclosed £ .... (cheques should be made payable to 'BRF')

Please complete and return the Gift Aid declaration on page 140 to make your donation even more valuable to us.

Please charge my MasterCard / Visa with £ ....

Card no. ☐☐☐☐ ☐☐☐☐ ☐☐☐☐ ☐☐☐☐

Expires end ☐M ☐M ☐Y ☐Y   Security code ☐☐☐   Last 3 digits on the reverse of the card

We will use your personal data to process this order. From time to time we may send you information about the work of BRF Ministries. Please contact us if you wish to discuss your mailing preferences **brf.org.uk/privacy**

Please return this form with the appropriate payment to:
BRF Ministries, 15 The Chambers, Vineyard, Abingdon OX14 3FE
For terms and cancellation information, please visit brfonline.org.uk/terms.

Bible Reading Fellowship is a charity (233280) and company limited by guarantee (301324), registered in England and Wales

BRF Ministries

Inspiring people of all ages to grow in Christian faith

BRF Ministries is the home of Anna Chaplaincy, Living Faith, Messy Church and Parenting for Faith

As a charity, our work would not be possible without fundraising and gifts in wills.
To find out more and to donate,
visit brf.org.uk/give or call +44 (0)1235 462305